PRAISE FOR *IM*

"In this inspiring and practical boo[k] the power of embracing our God-given abilities and make an impact on the world. She shows us how to align our vision with God's and to live life with greater significance and purpose. I'm grateful for how Stephanie has already applied what she's written to our network of churches, making a difference in the lives of so many."

—ANDY STANLEY, AUTHOR, COMMUNICATOR, AND
SENIOR PASTOR OF NORTH POINT MINISTRIES

"This book is for anyone who is ready to imagine more for their life and take action toward their dreams. Stephanie shows readers how to identify their passions and find their unique path toward a fulfilling and joyful life."

—BOB GOFF, *NEW YORK TIMES* BESTSELLING
AUTHOR OF *DREAM BIG* AND *LOVE DOES*

"Stephanie continues to amaze me with her focus on three things: following your dreams, being your own boss, and serving others. She will inspire you to the same focus in your own life."

—CLARK HOWARD, NATIONAL CONSUMER
ADVISOR, *NYT* BESTSELLING AUTHOR OF *CLARK
HOWARD'S LIVING LARGE IN LEAN TIMES*, AND
HOST OF *THE CLARK HOWARD PODCAST*

"*Imagine More* invites you to tap into the visionary power of imagination through the powerful vehicle of prayer. Stephanie Nelson is living proof that when you talk and listen to God daily and diligently, He will speak to you through the dreams in your heart, giving you innovative ideas, courage, passion, and purpose to make an amazing difference in the world for Him."

—BECKY TIRABASSI, CO-PASTOR AT VIEWPOINT
CHURCH, AUTHOR OF *LET PRAYER CHANGE
YOUR LIFE*, AND FOUNDER OF THE LEAD HOUSE

"Stephanie Nelson's *Imagine More* book is a fun, uplifting read. She demonstrates how to take a simple idea and overcome doubters and roadblocks with charm and determination, leading to her remarkable success. Stephanie is generous in highlighting the impact of others on her journey. Her positive approach is infectious and shows you how the power of accepting help, combined with the power of giving help to others, can create a joyful, connected community."

—BARBARA DUFFY, RETIRED EXECUTIVE DIRECTOR
AT NORTH FULTON COMMUNITY CHARITIES

"Jesus has so much more for you, and Stephanie Nelson is just the person to encourage you to go for it. Stephanie's experience, encouragement, and faith will guide you along your journey to imagine more by prompting you to utilize your passions and talents to make a difference in your own life, in this world, and in God's kingdom."

—LAURA L. SMITH, BESTSELLING AUTHOR OF
RESTORE MY SOUL AND *HOW SWEET THE SOUND*

"In this amazing book Stephanie provides a roadmap for not only understanding what's possible for your life but also for turning that possibility into a God-given reality. Based on her own story, Stephanie shares the lessons she learned so you can imagine more for your life!"

—BRETT R. SMITH, PHD, PROFESSOR OF
ENTREPRENEURSHIP AT MIAMI UNIVERSITY AND
FOUNDING DIRECTOR OF L.I.F.E. (LEADING THE
INTEGRATION OF FAITH & ENTREPRENEURSHIP)

"Listening to that nagging feeling that you have more potential to live out takes real courage. Stephanie knows this because she has experienced it. And she invites you to take the risk to believe with a faith that can ground you and inspire you to do more than you ever knew possible."

—HEATHER PENNY, PHD, AUTHOR OF
THE LIFE YOU'RE MADE FOR

"An encouraging and uplifting read, and a wonderful story of how one person can make a difference in the world. Stephanie has a true heart for helping people. Her message is clear: we find our greatest success in serving others."

—DAVID DINGESS, AUTHOR OF *THE CHILD OF GOD* AND *WHERE ARE YOU?*

"Stephanie Nelson and her husband, Dave, have truly inspired me to imagine more. Her vision, passion, commitment, and generosity have helped bring the dream of East Cobb Church into reality in ways I never imagined. With wisdom and authenticity, Stephanie shares her own journey as an entrepreneur, offering invaluable insights on how to leverage your natural abilities to make a lasting impact in the world. I hope you enjoy this story of a life well lived and decide to go live one of your own—all for others' good and God's glory."

—JAMEY DICKENS, LEAD PASTOR AT EAST COBB CHURCH

IMAGINE MORE

IMAGINE MORE

Do What You Love, Discover Your Potential

STEPHANIE NELSON

FOUNDER OF COUPON MOM

NELSON
BOOKS

An Imprint of Thomas Nelson

Imagine More

© 2023 by Stephanie Nelson

Published in Nashville, Tennessee, by Nelson Books, an imprint of Thomas Nelson. Nelson Books and Thomas Nelson are registered trademarks of HarperCollins Christian Publishing, Inc.

Thomas Nelson titles may be purchased in bulk for educational, business, fundraising, or sales promotional use. For information, please email SpecialMarkets@ThomasNelson.com.

Unless otherwise noted, Scripture quotations are taken from The Holy Bible, New International Version®, NIV®. Copyright © 1973, 1978, 1984, 2011 by Biblica, Inc.® Used by permission of Zondervan. All rights reserved worldwide. www.Zondervan.com. The "NIV" and "New International Version" are trademarks registered in the United States Patent and Trademark Office by Biblica, Inc.®

Scripture quotations marked ESV are taken from the ESV® Bible (The Holy Bible, English Standard Version®). Copyright © 2001 by Crossway, a publishing ministry of Good News Publishers. Used by permission. All rights reserved.

Any internet addresses, phone numbers, or company or product information printed in this book are offered as a resource and are not intended in any way to be or to imply an endorsement by Thomas Nelson, nor does Thomas Nelson vouch for the existence, content, or services of these sites, phone numbers, companies, or products beyond the life of this book.

ISBN 978-1-4002-4404-1 (eBook)
ISBN 978-1-4002-4401-0 (TP)

Library of Congress Control Number: 2023939207

Printed in the United States of America
23 24 25 26 27 LBC 5 4 3 2 1

With love to our sons, David and Chris.
I pray you will always Imagine More,
because God can do immeasurably more
than all we ask or imagine. (Ephesians 3:20)

Contents

CONTENTS

Introduction

IMAGINE MORE

You see people doing amazing things. Sure, you'd love to be like them, but you can't. You didn't go to an Ivy League school, and you don't have extra money. You can't sing or dance. You're tied down with real-life responsibilities like a job that pays the bills and kids to raise. Doing the exciting things you may have dreamed about when you were younger isn't realistic anymore.

But you have a nagging feeling that there must be more. That you haven't reached your life's full potential yet. We all see someone we know hitting it out of the park with a business they built or helping countless people with a charitable cause they started. They don't appear smarter than we are; some people just lead charmed lives, it seems. Sometimes we envy them, even when we have so much to be thankful for in our own lives. We may not envy their financial success but we envy their sense of purpose. They've found their ideal path.

You may have talents and skills you haven't used in a

while. You've thought of new projects that interest you, but there's no time to fit anything else in your busy life. So you settle and accept and remember to be thankful for all that you have. Sometimes you feel like you're watching life from the sidelines, but you can't imagine how you'd ever be able to get in the game.

Does any of that feel familiar? If you are fulfilled and have found your purpose, that's fantastic. But if not, if you are reading this book to find more, I know you can. You are never too young or too old to pursue a new journey perfectly suited to your abilities and desires. You can discover God's purpose and plan for making a difference in this world right where you are now, in the context of your current situation. You may be surprised at where He can take you while you are still meeting your current responsibilities—even if you don't have the degree or the dollars. Far more is possible than you can even imagine; you just have to start looking and dreaming. God doesn't want us to be watching from the sidelines. And that's why, when you find your purpose, you will experience the excitement, fun, and true joy of knowing you are doing exactly what God wants you to do.

This book will help you discover God's ideal plan for you. I'll share practical strategies for discovering and implementing your new ideas. You can build a successful business or a charitable cause, even while being a parent with young children or a busy executive. Our plans may take more time to jumpstart because of time constraints, but as it turns out, that will probably be the perfect timing. God won't ask us to choose between the life situations we love and the dreams He gives us. It can all be one life path.

We may not have extra money or the necessary technical background or the professional experience to start a business. If a company were hiring a person to do the jobs we dream of, we may not be qualified. Fortunately, God isn't limited by practical details like those. He knows our hearts and desires and He can fill in the rest. This book is a compilation of what worked for me, whether I discovered these things myself or was tipped off by someone who was further along on the journey. My hope is that these ideas will help you realize that you can make a difference in your part of the world too. And when you do, you'll experience the peace and satisfaction of knowing you're making a difference while doing what comes most naturally to you. I am excited for you to find your unique path, and I'm looking forward to helping you get started.

God's big plan for you right now may not be to start a new charity, launch a business, or write a book. His plan for each of us is to learn to love Him and each other better. You may choose to do that by starting a big initiative or project. You can also do that right where you are by being more intentional in your everyday life. Finding your purpose may be closer than you think.

What if you could partner with God to help find your unique purpose? Instead of asking God what He can do for us, we could ask God what we could do for Him. We can ask God to use us for a greater purpose. You may not know exactly what it is right now, but that's okay. God already knows what it is—and He's just waiting for you to ask.

1

The Coupon Mom Story

"I know the plans I have for you," declares the
LORD, "plans to prosper you and not to harm
you, plans to give you hope and a future."

—JEREMIAH 29:11

Nearly twenty-one years ago, author Becky Tirabassi came to speak at our church. She had written a great book called *Let Prayer Change Your Life*, so having the opportunity to hear her speak in person was exciting. Her talk was inspiring, but who knew that it would be the first step in my own exciting twenty-year journey? Becky encouraged the audience to pray about how God could use what we loved to do to help others. She said that no matter how trivial our favorite pastime might seem, if we could find a way to use it to help people, that would be God's exciting plan for our life.

Becky's talk led me to the idea of using my favorite pastime: shopping with grocery coupons. We've all been stuck in line behind someone at the grocery store who was using a big stack of coupons. After several beeps from the cash register and waiting for an eternity, the shopper paid the cashier a few cents and walked out of the store with a cart of groceries. Their savings may be impressive, but you wouldn't want to be the one holding up a grocery line with people giving you irritated looks, which is why most people aren't interested in learning how to use coupons. Even if they save you a little money, the embarrassment of being one of those strange coupon people wouldn't be worth it.

DISCOVERING MY CALLING

As you can see, trying to convince the world to use grocery coupons to help their families save money was going to be an uphill climb. But coupons were a favorite pastime of mine, so that was the starting point.

I started praying every morning for God to show me how to use the knowledge of couponing to help others. It was a fun game if you knew how to do it well. Regardless of whether using coupons was embarrassing or not, you could buy good groceries at virtually no cost when you knew the best way to use coupons. When families are struggling to make ends meet, and kids are going hungry because their parents don't have enough money to buy groceries, why wouldn't the world want to

THERE HAD TO BE A WAY TO USE THIS SKILL TO HELP PEOPLE.

know how to do this? I thought there had to be a way to use this skill to help people.

On day eleven of praying about this, our church bulletin included an appeal for donations for the local food pantry. The bulletin listed the most-needed food items, and every single one was a "coupon item." Best of all, it was our grocery store's Super Double Coupon Week. With a stack of coupons, sixty dollars of groceries for the food pantry cost me only ten dollars. That was my big lightbulb moment.

After delivering the groceries and seeing the people in the waiting room at the food pantry, everything changed. This was no longer a trivial hobby. Mothers like me with children like mine were waiting for a few bags of food to get through the week. It broke my heart. God showed me that buying food for charity was my new calling. After that I took my coupons to the store every day, bought the best coupon deals for charity, and delivered them to the food pantry with our two young sons in tow. It filled me with joy to do it, and I felt like God was right beside me. However, no matter how many groceries we brought, we couldn't keep up with the demand. There were just too many people who needed help, and one family certainly couldn't fix it all.

I learned that many food pantries were empty and turning away families in need. There had to be a way to teach others how to get free groceries for food pantries. We needed lots of people to learn how to do it. Ideally, we could teach the clients of the food pantry how to get free groceries with coupons too. They wouldn't be embarrassed to use coupons at grocery stores if it meant they could feed their families good food within their budget. We just had to find a way to bridge the gap between people knowing how to shop with coupons and their circumstances. They faced many challenges, including time constraints, transportation, childcare, and not being able to afford the Sunday newspaper that had the grocery coupons. Most of them worked more than one job while taking care of a family. How could they find the time to come to a coupon workshop? I decided to start with building a crew to help.

SPREADING THE WORD

Teaching neighbors and friends how to buy and donate free groceries with coupons was the next step, because far more families would be helped if we could multiply our donations. None of the women I approached knew how to do the coupon thing, but they were willing to learn for the good cause of feeding families in need. We sat around my kitchen table and held a Grocery Coupon University. We had lots of laughs as they realized this crazy thing worked. We could go into grocery stores with little pieces of paper we cut out of the newspaper and walk out with hundreds of dollars of free groceries with our combined efforts. It was like legal shoplifting. Yes, it was legal!

Handing coupons to a cashier isn't difficult, but figuring out the deals can be. It's a puzzle, matching up coupons with items that are on sale. Fortunately, that's what I could bring to our kitchen-table group. For some of us this grocery coupon puzzle is a mental challenge—a fun hobby. The grocery deals are the same across my entire state of Georgia, so in theory, only one person needed to figure out each week's deals if there was a way to share that information with others in a timely way.

At the time (it was 2000), there were old-fashioned snail-mail newsletters about how to save money on groceries, but nothing as specific as a list of the best deals at your own grocery store. Since prices and coupons change every week, you'd never be able to publish and distribute a paper newsletter quickly enough. Email newsletters made sense, but we didn't have any subscribers. The best idea would be to publish the information on a website and make it free to anyone who wanted to use it. Although starting a website seems obvious now, websites were still a relatively new thing, and they weren't easy to publish back then. But it was clear that if we had a website, we could teach far more people how to donate food to charity at no cost.

It made perfect sense. Rather than each person in the state having to figure out all these deals at their kitchen table, one person could figure them out and then *share* that information, at no cost, on a website. This was the key to teaching thousands of people how to buy free groceries for their families as well as for charity. We couldn't squeeze them all around my kitchen table, and we wouldn't need to do hundreds of coupon workshops.

Starting a website meant that someone would have to consistently spend hours a week figuring out the grocery deals and publishing them on the website. It was a big commitment, but it was clearly what we needed to do, and it actually sounded like a lot of fun to me. It didn't sound fun to anyone else, so that was the next decision. God could not have spoken to me more clearly, and He answered my prayer. He showed me exactly what could be done to use the grocery coupon system to help others. He never said it would be easy. It took thirty-plus hours of data entry a week for the next three years before I could afford to hire data entry help. It was honestly a labor of love, regardless of the hours of mind-numbing data entry. Fortunately, God's answer to my prayer was a clear vision that provided seemingly bottomless energy in those early years.

GOD'S ANSWER TO MY PRAYER WAS A CLEAR VISION THAT PROVIDED SEEMINGLY BOTTOMLESS ENERGY.

In early 2001 I launched a website and made that commitment. The site cost twenty dollars a year, started with dial-up internet, and we called it Cut Out Hunger. The website published lists of the best coupon deals at the grocery stores every week, which could be useful to millions of people in our state if they knew it was available. I just had to get people to understand what this website provided. The website's tagline was "Cut your grocery bill in half and feed the hungry too."

There was no specific plan. It was just an idea that I truly believed could help the world by feeding the hungry. In the beginning my only plan was to convince a company or organization with resources that they should take the idea off my hands and run with it. That's right—the only path to success seemed to be giving the idea away to someone more capable. With no experience running a website, with no extra money for staffing a business, and with two small children to take care of, I thought this idea would be wasted in my incompetent hands. The idea was fabulous, but someone more qualified needed to run with it.

Have you ever felt like you weren't the person for the job? We've all felt that way. But sometimes we're the only ones available, so we don't have a choice. We just have to get to work.

My pre-mom career was being a salesperson for ten years, so approaching people wasn't hard. Executives in the grocery industry and coupon industry as well as leaders of hunger organizations agreed to meet and hear my pitch. Some liked the idea and appreciated my enthusiasm but politely explained that it didn't fit with their business plan. Others were less than polite and hated the idea! Some offered their help in small ways that were a big help to my efforts. The idea touched them personally and they wanted to help. But no one would take it on as their project.

The only option left for me was to take small steps that didn't cost money. I taught free workshops to get the word out. Civic organizations and church groups invited me to speak at their meetings, and they spread the concept within their organizations. Local media outlets gave the website free press coverage. Our plan looked more like a maze than a clear road map, but we made a little progress each day. Some doors opened, and some slammed in my face. We just kept looking for new doors—because slammed doors lead to God's door.

REJECTION OPENS DOORS

Three years went by. It's a good thing I didn't know in the beginning how long I'd be working without any help. That's probably why God won't give us a crystal ball; we don't need to be discouraged. The website needed staff—help with data entry, advertising, a website designer, a publicist, and a programmer. That required money. Similar sites in other states were charging subscription fees starting at sixty dollars a month. That didn't work for my dream. The goal was to maximize users who would then donate food to charity; the website audience couldn't be limited just to people willing to pay sixty dollars a month. Other startup website owners were spending their life savings to try to launch their websites. That wasn't an option either. There were some ads on my website that earned a few hundred dollars a month. But it would take millions of users to make enough money to grow a national effort with those ads. It had already taken three years to get a few thousand users, so getting to millions of users seemed impossible.

I had one more option. Our church's accountant offered to take us on as a pro bono client. He said if the website was approved for nonprofit 501(c)(3) status, it could get government grants to fund its operation. This would obviously be a great use of taxpayers' money, so I gratefully took him up on his generous offer. He had his firm put together a four-inch-thick application, he kindly paid the hefty application fee, and I waited. A couple months later, the IRS examiner called to let me know the application was rejected. I thought this was the last hope for getting this great idea off the ground, so her answer didn't make any sense. She felt sorry for me as I explained my plight, but she didn't budge. She explained that the site helped people save money, which was providing a personal financial benefit to people. She thought the financial benefit to the site users disqualified the site from being a nonprofit. If we took the weekly grocery deals information for shoppers out, and only included the idea of donating food to charity, the IRS could approve it.

Unfortunately, if I made that change, the website would help far fewer people. Compromising the website's content for the sake of getting government dollars did not seem like God's intention at all. The best way to attract more people was to help them save money on their own groceries, and then the site would lead them to the logical idea of donating extra items to charity. Plus, food pantry clients and food stamp recipients were using the website to stretch their limited budgets, just as we had hoped they would. Taking the personal savings part out wasn't an option—it would cripple the vision. So I did not agree to the IRS's requirements and accepted that the website would not be a tax-exempt, nonprofit organization to receive grants and donations. I would have to find another way to fund and grow the website.

The IRS rejection felt like the last straw. Why wouldn't God want this idea to grow and help people? I had worked hard for three years. Many businesses give up in less time than that when they don't make a profit. I wasn't trying to make a profit and didn't even expect to make a salary. I needed funding to hire staff. Otherwise, it was unlikely the website could ever grow to its potential. It just didn't seem fair.

Ultimately the website was funded through ads from

Google AdSense, but that ad product wasn't even offered until 2003. When we applied for 501(c)(3) nonprofit status in 2002, we could imagine no means of financial support other than donations and grants. The vision seemed so clear, so good, so helpful to people who desperately needed help. On top of that, our accountant said that in all of his years of practice, I was the only client to be rejected by the IRS. The only client ever. Hard to believe.

Can you think of a rejection that was so painful it caused you to give up? Has rejection ever seemed like a message from God that you were pursuing the wrong path? That's what the IRS rejection felt like. I thought this must have been God's clear message that the website wasn't His vision after all.

So I got on my knees and prayed for God to take away my drive and obsession with this project. My frustration was causing me to be angry and short-tempered with my family. That wasn't what God wanted. I would continue to provide the site for its current audience but would give up the goal of growing it and trying to spread the word about it. I prayed that God would help me be thankful for what it was and stop trying to force it to be more than that. I prayed that prayer at 9:30 on a Sunday night.

God isn't a genie in a bottle—we can't say magical words and expect Him to grant our wishes. But when we pray, regardless of what we say, He hears our hearts. The important part of prayer isn't the specific words, or even how God answers them. The important part is that we can go to Him, we can get on our knees, we can pour out our hearts to God. Isn't that what He wants from us? To come to Him as our trusted Father, to be honest with Him about our feelings and our struggles. Isn't that what we would want from our own children? Just doing this gave me a feeling of peace. God will do that trade every time: our problems for His peace.

As it turns out, God is bigger than the IRS. The next morning I didn't even turn on my computer. At about 9:30, a friend who worked with a PR agency called and said, "How'd you get Clark Howard to talk about your website on the radio today?" I didn't. Clark Howard is a national financial expert based in Atlanta. Everyone in Atlanta knows that Clark can't be bought, and if he recommends something, you can trust it's good. His recommendations are golden. The website traffic soared.

My friend said the next step should be to call local radio and TV shows to let them know Clark had endorsed the site and ask them to feature the website on their shows. They all said yes.

A few weeks later I went on *Good Day Atlanta*, my first live TV appearance. The segment demonstrated how to get a table filled with groceries for charity, absolutely free. Another guest on the show that day was impressed with the coupon system and thought it should be on national TV. He shared the name of a high-level *Good Morning America* producer and told me to call her. He said, "Tell her what you've got in thirty seconds or less." So I did.

GOOD MORNING AMERICA

The call from *Good Morning America* came a few months later. It was a dream come true. The segment was six minutes

on national TV with millions of viewers. Their team produced a professional shopping video with dramatic savings
results—and it was funny and entertaining. It turns out this
was an engaging TV topic, which ended up being the key to
its media success over the next several years.

The show's anchor ended the segment by asking about our
program's special angle. That was her signal for me to talk
about Cut Out Hunger. This was the dream come true—the
vision that had run through my mind a million times over the
past three years. This was the chance to say the words that
might get viewers' attention, which might make them find
their local food pantry and start donating food where they
lived all across the country. I'll never forget the words I shared
on that incredible day:

> One in five people go hungry in our country. Every week
> there are free grocery deals with coupons—and 99 per-
> cent of coupons are thrown away. Imagine how many
> food items we could donate with these coupons.
>
> We have an easy system to use coupons that is available
> at no cost. I've done the math. If every household donated
> one item to charity a week, we would wipe out hunger in
> our country.[1]

And the segment ended. It felt like jumping off a cliff
and being caught in God's arms. Everything was fine. The
website traffic went crazy.

Many viewers sent emails to the website. Some said,
"I've always used coupons but never thought to donate to
charity." Others said, "I've always donated food to charity

but never thought to use coupons." But I'll never forget the one that said, "I will probably never use a coupon in my life, but I'll always donate one item a week to charity." That one still gets me.

Before *GMA* the website earned about ten dollars a day from Google Ads. Roughly 5 percent of site users clicked on an ad, and Google paid me for every click. Because Google Ads provided valuable offers such as printable grocery coupons, the ads helped users save even more money. That ten dollars a day was enough to pay for the website's operational costs but not enough to hire any staffing help. All my spare time, still about thirty hours a week, was devoted to doing data entry—late into the night, early in the morning, and every minute our kids were in school.

The morning after the *GMA* segment, I went up to my computer and checked the revenue report for the website ads. Because thousands of new people had come to the website, we had far more clicks on our ads. In shock, I came down to the kitchen and said to my husband, "The website ads made $10,000 yesterday." The look on his face was priceless! My family always teased me good-naturedly about my coupon obsession. He wasn't making fun of me that day!

That $10,000 was a game changer for the website's growth. It enabled me to hire data entry help for the entire year. Having data entry staff freed up time for me to focus on growing the website with media appearances, writing articles, and speaking to more audiences.

The night of the *GMA* appearance, the producer called our home. She said, "Thank you for your persistence. That was our number one news story of the day across all ABC news shows. What else do you know about saving money? We want to have you back on."

GMA gave me a contract and paid me for each appearance. They created the name Coupon Mom. We stopped using Cut Out Hunger and bought the CouponMom.com domain name—it was much easier for people to understand and remember—for thirteen dollars. *GMA* featured seventeen Coupon Mom segments over the next three years. What seemed like a confusing maze of a journey was actually God's amazing journey.

WHAT IS YOUR DREAM?

Before we go any further, here's a question to consider. Do you have a dream, something you wonder and ruminate about? Even if it's something you've never admitted to anyone else. If you don't, why not? Perhaps you have already accomplished every single big thing you ever wanted to do, and if that's the case, congratulations! Bill Gates probably isn't reading this book, but if he is, he gets a pass. But maybe you don't think your big dream is remotely possible, so you don't let yourself think about it. And that's kind of sad.

If you do have something in mind, let yourself dream. It could come true, especially if you do something about it. Without a doubt people could experience more of their big dreams if they believed those dreams were possible. I'll be honest—I dreamed about going on TV with my coupon message because television appearances were the easiest and cheapest way to reach a lot of people. Remember, this was the early

2000s, before Facebook and Instagram were even invented, so social media was not an option. With no prior experience with TV, radio, or any other media outlet, there was no logical reason for me to dream about going on TV with my message. Even so, I practiced in the mirror and talked to a pretend TV audience while driving in the car. All the time.

The point of *Imagine More* is to prove that you can achieve your big dream. You can experience the wonder and beauty of helping people through your dream—in fact, you're supposed to. God has an incredible plan for you that

PEOPLE COULD EXPERIENCE MORE OF THEIR BIG DREAMS IF THEY BELIEVED THOSE DREAMS WERE POSSIBLE.

He's waiting for you to find. The great part is that you don't have to apply or train or ask permission. You can just start.

Do you have a dream? It can come true. We haven't met, but we are probably a lot alike because you're reading this book. You can be effective at just about anything and make a difference in God's economy. Some of us are skilled at coupons, which isn't exactly rocket science. But we learned that even a crazy idea can be used by God.

What comes easily to you? What do you love doing? It may be just a dream now, but catching that dream is the most important first step in starting your unique journey. You are the only one qualified to follow God's exciting plan for your life. He picked you.

Before that first *GMA* appearance, a local TV producer said this would be the defining moment of my experience. From here on, he said we would always think in terms of "before *GMA*" and "after *GMA*." It would change everything. He was right. The grocery coupon thing was a topic none of the TV producers understood but their viewers loved. At first I thought having my picture on my website and naming the site Coupon Mom seemed egotistical, but that's actually what people responded to. The producers said I was relatable and authentic. Their viewers were just like me. *GMA* didn't suggest media training. When I asked about it, they said no, just be yourself. Instead of making wardrobe suggestions, they told me to wear what I liked. Fortunately, I'd had all that practice with my pretend TV audience in the car!

GMA just wanted me to be myself. To talk about my favorite hobby. To give viewers practical information they could use. It's easy to be ourselves, and we are all more comfortable talking about what comes naturally to us. When you pursue your dream, you won't need to be anyone different than you are. God's pretty happy with what He created, so there's no need to mess with that.

Over a seven-year period I did fifty-five national TV appearances featuring our coupon system, as well as hundreds of local TV and radio interviews. The *Oprah Winfrey Show* even had me demonstrate the system to their viewers. The website went from a few thousand visits a month before the first national TV appearance on *GMA* to five million a month at its peak. It made more than enough money from ads to fund its own growth and staffing.

NEW ADVENTURES

My accountant said the best thing that ever happened was being rejected by the IRS! Who knew? Well, we can be pretty sure that God knew. He had something far better in store, which was impossible to see at the time of the IRS phone call. Keep that in mind. It's so important to remember that there is far more ahead than we could ever even imagine. "I know the plans I have for you," God tells us, "plans to prosper you and not to harm you, plans to give you hope and a future" (Jeremiah 29:11). He knows our hearts, and when we are aligned with God's will for us, with His dreams for us, unexpected and surprising things will happen.

Companies hired me to be a paid spokesperson. Who knew that was even a thing? The first deal? A dial-up internet company! Who could believe this was a career? It was fun to say simple, obvious things with great authority. It's fun to master looking into the camera and saying with a straight face, "The best way to save money on groceries is to make a shopping list." Seriously. They paid me to say brilliant things like that.

Everything was easy now—all doors opened and phone calls were always returned. And the best part was that coupons were working. People were saving money and donating to charity. Happy emails from site users poured in, and they filled me with joy. It felt too good to be true.

But it got better. Once free blog software became popular in 2010,[2] other women created their own coupon sites using our approach. Their sites also listed grocery deals and promoted giving food to charity. Pretty soon there were hundreds of other coupon moms across the country.

I'll be honest. Those new coupon moms coming on the scene made us a little nervous. They were getting on TV. They were young, hip, sassy, and fun—serious competition. I was concerned that they would damage my business.

And that is the biggest example of how wrong we can be when we think we know what's going to happen in the future. Honestly, we really don't know. Just ten years earlier I could hardly get anyone to agree to use coupons, and I didn't know how in the world to teach millions of people how to use my website. I certainly never dreamed that a bunch of people would copy the concept and be new coupon moms getting on TV shows that reached millions of people too. Our publicist was very concerned, and she thought it was the end of our fifteen minutes of fame. That would have been okay, because I'd certainly had more than my fair share of positive experiences and success by that point. I could pass the baton to these younger women, especially when they shared the same goal. To be honest, it was a lot of fun to sit back and watch them demonstrate their unbelievable coupon savings on TV. That was my kind of TV!

Well, they say all boats rise when the river rises. Those other coupon moms created far more interest in coupons, with exponential media exposure. There were dozens of them going on local and national TV all across the country. As a result, they dramatically grew the industry. Millions of new coupon users went to the internet to find grocery coupon websites, and our business more than doubled the year they all started. We had the highest-traffic year ever as a result of their appearances. Those women taught their communities how to save and donate to charity. They taught me that we have a lot in common with our competitors and that we should really be friends. They earned incomes while staying home with their kids. Some of those women became millionaires. Everyone won—especially the shoppers who were saving money by using all these free, easy websites. Millions of families saved money and donated food to charity. This exceeded every single one of my crazy dreams. In God's economy, everybody can win.

A highlight for me was speaking at a conference for coupon moms, as the experienced pioneer. It was like we had found our tribe. No single company could have done what the combined efforts of an army of coupon moms did. A coupon company executive asked me, "How does it feel to have created a cottage industry?" But I didn't create it. I never even saw that coming. That's a plan only God could have dreamed up.

> IN GOD'S ECONOMY, EVERYBODY CAN WIN.

Going on *GMA* wasn't the defining moment. Getting on my knees and giving it up to God was the defining moment. That's when I came to the end of myself and my limited plan and got to watch what happens when we let God take over. When we give up, we let God show up.

People might see all this as luck and good timing. They might see these turning points as coincidences. They are wrong. God had His hand in this—He was so dramatic about it. When I prayed on my knees and asked Him to take away my unhealthy drive to make my idea succeed, He was probably thinking that drive was what He was trying to use. He was waiting for me to follow His lead. It's not a coincidence that Clark Howard talked about the website just twelve hours after I prayed, when I'd been working at this for three years. It's not a coincidence that a person who knew the top *GMA* producer happened to be standing next to me in the wings of *Good Day Atlanta* for just fifteen minutes.

It's not even a coincidence that the IRS examiner who called misinterpreted the law. As it turned out, her assessment was incorrect. Our website offered information that helped shoppers save money if they chose to use it. Countless nonprofit organizations provide a personal financial benefit to their audience with various types of financial training, information, and direct financial support, so her rationale probably would not have held water if we had appealed it. Fortunately, we decided not to appeal. Since we were a private company we could have advertising on the website. Due to the site's high traffic over time, our advertising revenue was much higher than government grants would have been, and we didn't need to spend time trying to raise financial support. The advertising revenue provided the money we needed to staff and grow without charging our audience a subscription fee. The last thing we wanted to do was take money from a family who was struggling financially. I'm not judging the businesses that use the subscription approach, but it just didn't feel right for us. My husband and I had all we needed. We are glad that as a private company we have paid income tax to the government all these years, rather than taking money from the government. We didn't need to compete for funding with the very nonprofits we were trying to help. The website revenue even allowed us to donate generously to other nonprofits every year.

We are so thankful for this story, for this journey that God unfolded over the past twenty years. It taught us so many lessons that I will share here, and which I hope will help you as you begin your next journey.

Now I dream about encouraging people to find and start their journeys. I want to help you figure out how to use what you love to help others. Let's discover God's exciting plan for your life. If He can do something with the idea of grocery coupons and a woman who had no technology experience and no money, what could He do with you and your idea?

What is your story? Is there something you love to do? Pray about how God can help you use it to help others and start your own wonderful journey.

WHAT I LEARNED

Your journey is a marathon, not a sprint. It's made up of many small steps, and they each may take time. The joy is in the experiences along the way, not just in reaching the ultimate goal.

Be you. Be authentic. You'll be most successful if your work fits who you are and what you believe in. You'll know if it doesn't fit—you'll be able to feel it. Catch yourself if that happens and get back to being your authentic self. Don't get pulled off the track to please someone else or to create a different impression.

Own your dream, even if you don't feel capable of

reaching it. You're the one with the vision; you're the one with the dream. It's easier to learn new skills to do the work or find people to work alongside you than it is to expect someone else to carry your vision to the finish line. Don't give your dream away to someone you think is more capable. You can do it. God picked you.

Find Your Bold Vision

2

Jesus looked at them and said, "With man this is
impossible, but with God all things are possible."

—MATTHEW 19:26

Congratulations! You've decided to help change the world
in a positive way by doing something you love to help
others. At this point you might not be clear on exactly how
to do that.

When we're wondering what to do, the best one to ask
for advice is the One who created us. He's really familiar
with our abilities. Be honest with God and ask Him what
He has in mind for you. Ask Him to help you identify the
unique skills and talents you can use to help others. Ask
anything. Prayer is private, and it's impossible to embarrass
ourselves with God. Be honest about what you love to do the
most, even if it seems insignificant. Trust Him to give you a
lightbulb moment.

What came to mind for me was using grocery coupons,

even though coupons weren't exactly rocket science. In fact, in the year 2000 couponing was a very unpopular activity, and coupon redemptions were extremely low. Even so, using coupons turned out to be the skill God used on my path, even if the world didn't understand it yet. So don't underestimate your skills or abilities, because God can work with anything. When we align our specific skills with our genuine desire to make a difference in the world, we'll be on our way to discovering our bold vision. Pray about it every day and see what happens.

GOD CAN WORK WITH ANYTHING.

What is it that you really love to do? Don't limit yourself based on what you think others would consider worthy of changing the world. God's economy doesn't always seem logical, so you don't have to start with a logical idea. Just start with what you love and go from there. Make a list of all kinds of things you enjoy doing. You can help people doing just about anything if it's something you love to do.

You may know what your abilities are, but perhaps you don't know exactly what your passion is. You'd like to help others, but you're not even sure who you could help. You know there are plenty of people in need of food, shelter, friendship, encouragement, love—the list goes on. Maybe you're just not sure where to start looking, and you're not sure what worthy cause really sparks your passion.

Ultimately, it's people we want to help. It's people we want to love. Pastor Andy Stanley, lead pastor of North

Point Ministries and bestselling author, says we should ask ourselves the question, "What breaks your heart? What makes you cry?"[1] That tells us who or what we care most about helping. That's a good start.

IDENTIFYING YOUR PASSIONS

Blake Mycoskie, the founder of TOMS Shoes, has practical tips about how to find your passion. Here are three questions he likes to ask people who are not sure what their passions are:

1. If you did not have to worry about money, what would you do with your time?
2. What kind of work would you want to do?
3. What cause would you serve?

Once you answer these questions, you'll have a good idea of what your passion is.[2]

The fun part of this process is that it gets you to pay attention. You're waiting for a brainstorm, a sign, a lightbulb moment. It could be something someone says or something another person is doing. Pay attention to what's going on around you. It's so easy for us to sleepwalk through our days and routines, missing all kinds of interesting things going on. This stage of the process wakes us up to the possibilities and gets us to pay closer attention to the people around us.

There are a couple of approaches to finding your bold vision. You can begin by asking what activities you like to do and then find a way to help people through doing them, as Blake Mycoskie suggests. Or, as Andy Stanley suggests, you can start with who you'd love to help—what breaks your heart—and figure out how to use your abilities to meet that need.

I started with what I loved to do, without a vision of who that would help. But knowing what we love to do is a first step to finding who to help. I didn't say "I want to help feed the hungry," but once we delivered those first bags of groceries to the food pantry, my heart broke when I saw mothers like me with children like mine waiting for the donated food. Perhaps God's strategy was to get me to the food pantry to feel their need. The strong emotional connection that sparked my passion to start helping would not have happened if I had dropped the food off at an impersonal food collection bin. God had a plan in sending me there.

Finding and being able to articulate your bold vision is a crucial first step in God's exciting plan for your life. It may seem outrageous and impossible, but that's good. If you set a really high bar and only get halfway, that's further than hitting a low bar. God likes high bars.

GOD LIKES HIGH BARS.

How do you know if you've hit on your bold vision? It's like falling in love. You can't think about anything else, you work it into every conversation, and you dream about future events that will further your vision. Just thinking about it is exciting. When I first heard Becky Tirabassi, the author of *Let Prayer Change Your Life*, her passion for inspiring others to pray about everything overflowed from her. It was clear she was passionate about helping others understand the power of prayer. Not because she felt she should, but because she couldn't help it. Today, more than twenty years later, she is still on fire with her bold vision!

Seeing someone's passion shows the rest of us what a bold vision feels like. It's not lukewarm; it's not a project we dread. It's so clear to us that we can't help but share it. After hearing Becky, I knew I wanted to experience that passion and find my purpose too. This is your dream, not necessarily your day job (yet). You have nothing to lose at this point and there's no performance review. You can be as audacious and outrageous as you want to be—it's your vision. Even if you think there's no possible way you could achieve it, go ahead and cast the vision you'd love to see happen. Don't limit God—He's not limiting you. Go big.

Damali Mirembe was orphaned at the age of ten in Uganda, along with her siblings and cousins, when all their parents died of AIDS. She is thankful that they were all placed together in a Ugandan orphanage run by a Christian married couple from the United States. The couple provided excellent care to the children, but Damali says the greatest gift the children received was learning about Jesus. As a result, she had a dream of starting an orphanage when she was an adult.

With no identified source of funding, her dream was especially big and audacious. She simply bought a few cribs one day and started taking abandoned babies into her home. By faith these humble beginnings have exploded into an entire ministry that now cares for more than one hundred children; runs three children's homes, four schools, and eight churches;

and spreads love in the three communities in which the orphans live. Damali's work and her faith have permanently changed not only the lives of the people she serves but also the lives of the people who have come to know and support her ministry. She's one of those ordinary people who partnered with God to do extraordinary, world-changing work.[3]

Although I didn't write it down, my bold vision ran around in my mind all day long. While driving in the car or doing my household chores, it was always there. When you hit on your bold vision, it may keep you awake at night. It will motivate you to do the tedious work and mind-numbing tasks necessary to keep the project going. For the first few years there was no one to do those tasks for me, so all my spare time was spent on the work. And the vision never faded. There were plenty of challenges and rejection, but a strong vision can survive all those bumps in the road. That's what bold vision is—unmistakable, unrelenting, and enduring. What was the big vision that captivated my thoughts? Every food pantry in the country overflowing with more than enough food to provide for every person in need. That's right, my vision was to wipe out hunger in America with grocery coupons.

You've probably already guessed, but that didn't happen. The website did not single-handedly wipe out hunger in America. Not even close. But what did happen was so much bigger than what would have happened by settling on a more realistic vision. A realistic goal would have been something like increasing food donations from the school food drive by 10 percent a year. That would have been a noble goal, it would have been a worthy contribution, and it would most likely have been achievable. But we can do better than that. Be outrageous and see what happens.

When we talk about vision, we're not talking about fancy mission statements and a long list of goals and strategies. Don't let yourself get overwhelmed with the magnitude of your big vision. You probably won't even have to write it down; you'll just see it. That's probably why they call it *vision*! You can take a couple of steps and make a little bit of progress each day. You can write a long-term plan, a short-term plan, or just keep a list of ideas and achievable tasks and give yourself credit for your daily progress. The overall twenty-year journey with Coupon Mom ended up being a big thing. But I never did a big thing at once. I just did a couple of little things each day that added up to a big thing over time. How do you eat an elephant? One bite at a time.

PURSUING YOUR VISION

Once you've landed on a vision, you can start trying strategies to move toward it. Strategies are simply tasks and processes, and you can modify them as needed, but your vision is fixed because you need a North Star. This means starting with the end in mind. Your strategies are simply the many different paths to get to the vision and are likely to change with time, circumstances, and results as you go along. Be willing to change your approach if necessary. That's super important. Don't become fixated on your specific strategies if they're not working. Remember, this is a process. Your initial strategies may not be exactly what gets you to your goal, but they will get you out of the starting gate. Keep in mind that what comes easily to you may be harder for others to understand, so testing your idea with actual people is helpful.

Once you have an idea, consider how to communicate it to your intended audience. When I first thought of teaching other shoppers how to use coupons to buy food for charity, I typed up a step-by-step document explaining how to figure out the best grocery deals each week, how to organize coupons, and the types of items to buy for charities. It was a simple presentation, but it gave me a starting point. Then I invited groups of women to my home to teach them using this document.

Sitting with typical grocery shoppers around our kitchen table taught me why using grocery coupons was difficult for some people and how to make it easier. It taught me how to simplify the process. I learned that most shoppers found figuring out the grocery deals far too confusing. If someone could figure out what the coupon deals were at every store each week, and all the shoppers needed to do was follow a list, they were happy to buy items for charity. If I hadn't tested my idea with real shoppers in the very beginning, I never would have discovered the real benefit I could offer—figuring out the grocery deals for everyone else. They didn't understand it, they didn't want to do it, and I thought it was fun. Perfect!

My work was cut out for me (pun intended). By figuring out the best coupon deals each week and posting them on our website, I ensured that anyone could easily save money. While buying food for charity, my friends discovered they could also save big on their own families' groceries. Those shoppers taught me that we could attract more people to the idea of buying food for charity if we made it easy for them to save on all their groceries. Our logical tagline was "Cut Your Grocery Bill in Half and Feed the Hungry Too."

The website response grew as visitors started saving dramatically for their own families and were happy to donate extra items to charity in exchange for the website's service. The media loved it, since they knew their audiences cared about saving money, the concept worked, and the site was free. Fortunately, the main expense was my time, and it was the best hobby I'd ever had. I loved it.

Generous press coverage spread our message. People across the state started using CouponMom.com. I received many heartfelt messages from people struggling financially, who thanked us for helping their family make ends meet. This was working! It was helping people of all income levels, which was very exciting. Many of our site users were low-income households, and they reported being able to stretch their grocery budget much further with our service. It's like the saying, "Give a man a fish and he eats for a day. Teach him to fish and he eats for the rest of his life." This website was teaching people to fish.

We made it easy to learn without having to attend a coupon workshop. It fit into my life as a busy mother, because being away from home to teach workshops wasn't possible. As you formulate the ideas to make your bold vision a reality, be honest with yourself about what fits in the context of your real life. If you burden yourself with an unrealistic workload, you won't be able to sustain it. Your bold vision can be compatible with the life you want to live. Life balance is important, even when you're trying to change the world!

A friend of mine retired from her teaching job when she had her first child, but she missed working with young students. In time she started a tutoring service from her home. Her mother came over for a couple hours in the afternoon to enjoy her grandchild, and my friend was able to teach students in a way that fit into her lifestyle. The students and their parents were happy, the grandmother was happy, and my friend enjoyed the balance between her professional and personal life.

HELPING OTHERS WITH THEIR VISION

When our website started gaining traction, the most exciting messages were from former food-pantry clients who were donating free food to charity themselves by using coupons. One woman said, "This was our best Christmas ever. For the first time in my life we were able to take two bags of groceries to the church food drive like everyone else does." These are the types of messages that will fill you with joy and keep you motivated to work harder. You'll find you're helping people you hadn't expected to help. Others may follow your lead and start doing similar efforts to help where they live. Your initial effort may be a seed that grows everywhere.

In your efforts to identify your true passion, you may discover others who have a vision that inspires you. You may not want to lead a charge, but you're excited about helping get another person's vision off the ground. If that resonates with you, reach out to leaders you see and offer to help with the skills you can offer.

Ginger is a director of a non-profit organization that helps children. She is passionate about assisting and protecting children who have been victims of abuse. Although her organization does incredible work, its fundraising efforts needed support. Ed had recently retired from his position as a senior executive with

YOUR INITIAL EFFORT MAY BE A SEED THAT GROWS EVERYWHERE.

a large corporation. He met Ginger through a friend and recognized an opportunity to help her. He volunteered to lead the board and recruited well-connected leaders in the community as board members. His wife, Nancy, took on the charge of leading committees to plan large fundraising events. Donations from businesses and foundations began pouring in. Ed and Nancy didn't need to start a charity to make a difference. They hitched their wagon to Ginger, who needed their experience and skill sets, and thus they helped someone else's dream.

We're very thankful for the many who came beside us to launch our program. Their contributions were even more important than mine. Once it was possible to hire women to do the thirty weekly hours of data entry, I could travel around the country to promote Coupon Mom. If they hadn't been doing their work every day, our service would have nothing to offer. If our publicist hadn't done her work of arranging media interviews, we wouldn't have been able to spread our message. If our developer hadn't optimized our website so it could withstand high-traffic spikes resulting from media appearances, it would have crashed, and no one would have been able to use the website at all. Each person knew that they were major participants in Coupon Mom's success and were proud of their contributions. One of the best parts of the entire experience was working with these wonderful people.

Being part of a team that is making a difference is every bit as rewarding as starting a new initiative. As you are looking for your bold vision for God's exciting plan for your life, don't rule out hitching your wagon to someone else's project. You could be exactly who they need to help make their vision a reality.

WHAT I LEARNED

Be honest about what you love to do. Even if you can't think of a way to help yet, you're an expert at your favorite topics, and that will make your work easy and enjoyable. Make a list of what you love to do, and don't eliminate any ideas in the beginning.

What breaks your heart? Is there a group of people, a cause, or a topic that you genuinely care about? Look into ways to help, either by starting a new initiative or by joining an existing group. Get involved or personally connected. Being able to envision making a difference with a group or cause you really care about will keep you motivated, even during difficult challenges.

Pay attention. Start being more aware as you wait and watch for your lightbulb moment or for an answer to your prayer to find your bold vision. It may be a conversation, an article, a news story, or even your church bulletin, where my idea came from. It may be right in front of you one day, and you don't want to miss it.

3

Discover Your Superpower

His master replied, "Well done, good and faithful
servant! You have been faithful with a few things;
I will put you in charge of many things."

—MATTHEW 25:23

As you get started on your bold vision, your new project, or your new calling, it's worth spending time to figure out what your superpower is. Other terms for *superpower* may be *spiritual gifts*, *talents*, or *skills*. Your superpower is whatever comes easily to you, pulls you off the couch, propels you forward into action, and gets you energized.

Over thirty years ago I worked for Janis Milham, my favorite boss ever. During her decades-long career she advanced to division president of a multibillion-dollar corporation before she retired to become an executive coach. Her resume might suggest her superpower was being a ruthless, competitive executive to rise so highly in the ranks. But that's not it. Janis had the rare ability to connect with people personally, to genuinely care about their emotional well-being, and to help them succeed professionally. Working for Janis just one year changed the trajectory of my career, because she helped develop my weaknesses into strengths when the easier strategy may have been to replace me. Simply put, her superpower was that she truly cared about people. By combining that with business skills, she rose as a strong leader who impacted thousands of lives while delivering strong financial results for the company.

IDENTIFY YOUR SUPERPOWER

Maybe you've taken a spiritual gifts inventory or a personality assessment that has provided insight into what your particular skills are. Or maybe you have a pretty good idea of what your strengths are based on past experiences. Do you know what your superpower is? Have people told you what they think it is? You may be surprised when you start exploring how you spend your time, what you like to dream about, and what others see as your superpower.

Ask those who know you best what they think your talents and strengths are. For example, at the beginning of the Coupon Mom journey, a speaker at the prayer seminar asked, "What do you love to do that can help people?" She said that once we'd figured out how to use what we loved to do to help others, we would have landed on God's exciting plan for our lives.

I thought my superpower, the thing that was fun and came easily, was using grocery coupons to get free groceries.

I asked God every day to reveal how I could use that to help people, and the path toward the big dream began, step by step. For the next twenty years, God showed me how to use that skill, and it was an exciting journey. But when we rely on our own perspective in understanding ourselves, we can have a limited view. Later I was discussing gifts and talents with my sister and said my grocery coupon knowledge was my gift. She looked at me with a smile and said, "Yes, that is something you know how to do well; that's a skill. But that's not your gift. It's bigger than that. Your gift is helping people. You really like helping people."

As soon as she said that, it rang true. And when we think of helping people as a superpower, that is much more lasting and far-reaching than knowing how to use grocery coupons. Teaching grocery savings may not be my main profession forever, but helping people will always be in style. Our superpowers are much broader than the specific skills that come easily to us. There is an overarching ability behind that specific skill that is important to identify, because it could empower you in many specific projects.

> I ASKED GOD EVERY DAY TO REVEAL HOW I COULD USE MY SUPERPOWER TO HELP PEOPLE, AND THE PATH TOWARD THE BIG DREAM BEGAN, STEP BY STEP.

For example, you may be a corporate trainer for your employer in the telecommunications industry. So your first thought may be that you are skilled in telecommunications. Yes, you probably are. But an overarching ability may be that you are an excellent trainer, so you could teach many skills once you learn them yourself. And beyond being an excellent trainer, you are probably an excellent communicator, which opens up far more opportunities beyond teaching. Your superpower is being an excellent communicator. A communicator can be a speaker, an author, or the host of a podcast. Do you see why we call this skill your superpower? It's something bigger than you first realize, and it can lead to many options.

Do you have someone who knows you better than you know yourself? Who believes in you? Start with them. Ask what they think your skills, talents, and superpowers are. The people who love us see us through rose-colored glasses at times, and that gets us to reach higher. Love has a way of lifting us up and encouraging us to be the people our loved ones see. We can also let others know what their special gifts, talents, or superpowers are, encouraging them to help the world in more ways than they realized were possible.

We all have multiple skills, talents, and qualities. In fact, some of the qualities we have always viewed as negative may be exactly what will help us succeed in reaching our dreams. For example, I've always been a talker. Countless times in my childhood my parents would call me a chatterbox and tell me to stop talking. My dad wouldn't let me hang out with him and my brother when they were fishing because he said my chatting scared the fish away! It's always been fun for me to meet new people and ask all kinds of questions to get to know them. But you probably wouldn't want to sit next to me on an airplane. I try to catch myself when I'm talking too much, but if I don't, I can rely on a family member to do it for me.

So here's the funny thing. When Coupon Mom hit its stride, companies would approach me to do media interviews as a paid spokesperson. They would pay me well to work for them for one day. A typical day would be a satellite media tour, which involved standing in a TV studio and doing a series of news interviews about grocery savings for local TV stations around the country via satellite. The first interview would be at 6 a.m., and there would be twenty to twenty-five interviews throughout the day. The companies were thrilled! They hired me over and over again because they said I was so good at talking. Who even cares about fishing? That doesn't pay me a dime. Suddenly what had seemed a negative quality for years became a very good quality. It's all about context.

FROM DREAM TO REALITY

Keep in mind that your strong qualities may not be the ones your friends and family always appreciate, but those attributes may be helpful as you pursue your bold vision. Being persistent, tenacious, thoughtful, analytical, bold, forthright, quiet, or even talkative may be exactly what you need to succeed, even if those qualities are a little irritating to the people who spend their lives with you.

My stepfather said, "God gives you a glimpse of what you're doing to help, which encourages you to continue doing it. But He couldn't show you all of it, because you couldn't possibly handle it." As you begin hearing from people you are helping, their gratitude will fuel your excitement and energy. And your dream will become your reality.

Jesus told His followers parables—stories to illustrate a lesson. The parable of the talents in Matthew 25:14–30 tells of a master who went on a trip, and before leaving he gave his servants a total of eight talents, which was a significant amount of money. There were three servants, and he gave each an amount based on his abilities. The first servant received five talents, the second received two, and the third received one. When the master returned, he was pleased with the first two servants, who had put their talents to work and had doubled their value. But the third servant with one talent was afraid to lose his, so he buried it to keep it safe. The master was not pleased with this lack of initiative. At the very least, the servant could have invested the talent with a banker to earn interest. So the master took the third servant's one talent and gave it to the second servant, who had demonstrated that he knew how to put talents to work.

Many theologians interpret this story to mean that God gives us talents and abilities because He trusts us to put them to work and

> **GOD GIVES US TALENTS AND ABILITIES BECAUSE HE TRUSTS US TO PUT THEM TO WORK.**

make a contribution to the world. If we don't put the talents He gave us to work, He will take them away and give them to someone else. When we do use our talents for good, He will give us even more.

If we believe that God gave us talents and abilities, it is our responsibility to put them to work for the sake of helping others, loving others, and doing God's work. Being modest about our talents and not putting them to full use only deprives the world of the benefits we can provide. You may not believe your talents matter to anyone because they seem minor to you. You like to sing and are pretty good at it, but there are lots of great singers out there. Perhaps you love to paint pictures but wouldn't want to risk having your work rejected if you tried to sell the paintings. So you bury these talents. You sing in the shower, or you paint pictures for your mother.

There's nothing wrong with that, but God has bigger plans for you. I can't sing or paint, but I'm thankful others can. Listening to songs recorded by those who can sing is something I do every day. My home is filled with beautiful paintings by a very modest friend. Adding beauty to the world with your talent is a gift to those who will appreciate it. Any talent can become a gift when we put it to work. If God could figure out how using grocery coupons would help the world, don't you think He could figure out how to use your talents?

There is something very rewarding waiting for you if you use your superpower to help others. You can connect with the ones you're helping and have the fulfillment of hearing their gratitude for what you've offered. Their gratitude will lead you to have more gratitude to God for the wonderful path you've discovered. So don't wait. Start looking for your superpower and start following the path that is waiting for you.

WHAT I LEARNED

Think broadly. Try to view your skills and abilities from a larger perspective. Keep peeling back the layers to identify a broader ability as your superpower. The broader your ability, the more possibilities you have to find your best path to make a difference.

 Explore all areas. Don't limit your thinking to just your professional experience. You may be an attorney but in your spare time you love to read. You write insightful thoughts in your personal journal because you enjoy it. Perhaps you're an author and others could be helped with those inspirational thoughts. Throw out a wide net in your life to surface all the things you love to do and all the things that come easily to you. You may be surprised where a new path could take you with abilities you think of as relaxing pastimes. Your best superpower could be hidden in the most fun part of your life. Perhaps your fun pastime could be your full-time life purpose! Wouldn't that be great?

> ANY TALENT CAN BECOME A GIFT WHEN WE PUT IT TO WORK.

Help others discover their superpowers. You may have a friend or a relative who is in a job they hate, but they don't feel they can do anything else. Helping them think through what their abilities are beyond their specific job could help free them to do something they'd love. Encourage others by helping identify their superpowers and give them the confidence to discover and pursue God's purpose.

Finding Your Big Idea

We are God's handiwork, created in
Christ Jesus to do good works, which God
prepared in advance for us to do.

—EPHESIANS 2:10

S ara Blakely, the founder of Spanx, tells the story of being
a fax machine salesperson in the '90s in Reid Hoffman's
book *Masters of Scale*. It hit Sara one day—she said she felt
like she was in the middle of the wrong movie. She actually
wrote in her journal, "I want to invent a product I can sell to
millions of people that will make them feel good."[1]

Even if you don't know your specific idea, you can start
by writing down a sentence like Sara's. Ask yourself what
it is you want to do in the broad sense, which will help you
look for specific ideas as you move through your daily life.
My sentence was, "I want to figure out a way to help people
with my grocery coupon hobby." That's still broad, but it's
specific enough to pay attention to possible ideas, which is

exactly what happened. The *Wall Street Journal* refers to Sara's search as a "deliberate hunt for a transformative concept." Hoffman is quoted as saying, "You have to be actively looking for it."[2] As I was. As Sara was.

In 1997 Sara was getting dressed for a party and wanted to wear control-top pantyhose under her clothes but didn't want the pantyhose to show in her shoes. So she cut the feet off her pantyhose and had her lightbulb moment. The rest is history—although it didn't come easily. She believed in her idea and put her all into making it a reality. Hoffman says you need a bias toward action. "It wasn't just born because Sara came up with an idea. It was born because she decided to do something about it."[3]

People like Sara's story because she created a product that was practical in her life, she understood the product's benefits for women like her, and she knew they would love it. I think a person who invents something that masks cellulite should get a Nobel Prize! But her company is worth more than $1 billion, so that's probably better than a prize.

HOW TO FILTER INPUT

Years ago Sara spoke at a conference my husband and I attended. An important point she shared was that in the beginning, she didn't tell anyone about her idea. Not even friends and family. Her intuition told her it was a great idea, and she didn't need anyone telling her why it wouldn't work.[4]

Her advice rings true. In the beginning of the Coupon Mom project, anyone within earshot of me heard all about coupons. People who didn't use coupons, which was practically everyone, were happy to explain what a bad idea it was. Neighbors, friends, and even relatives laughed and shared all the reasons coupons didn't work for them. My mother-in-law was mortified because she felt the coupon system gave people the impression that her son didn't make enough money to support his family. Fortunately, their input didn't stop me from finding the people who liked the idea—but it did unnecessarily strain relationships. Keeping new ideas to yourself can help prevent unproductive negativity.

Another reason to keep your idea to yourself is because even though they may mean well, people who don't understand your idea can plant seeds of doubt in your mind. For example, you may have a great idea for a new product or service, and your friend will say, "Oh, someone else has already done that." Just because someone has done something similar to what you're doing doesn't mean your idea couldn't be better. The market segment may be large enough for plenty of similar options. What if the creators of Facebook had given up their idea because Myspace already existed? There was another social media site before Facebook, with significant investor support, called Friendster. Ever heard of that? You get my point. Don't internalize advice from people who don't understand your idea. You have a dream, and they can't see it like you can see it.

When we developed our coupon website, we knew we had to overcome

> **YOU HAVE A DREAM, AND THEY CAN'T SEE IT LIKE YOU CAN SEE IT.**

the obstacle of how tedious it was to cut out and organize coupons, which was why most people didn't use them. The traditional method required cutting out and filing two-hundred-plus newspaper coupons every week. Diligent coupon users would take their coupon collections shopping with them and search for specific coupons when they saw favorite items on sale in the store. It could take several hours a week in total, and this was the primary reason people said they gave up on coupons.

We developed a feature that made it easy for shoppers. We went to the stores, did hours of research to find the best sale items, and listed them on our website. If an item had a coupon available, we matched the coupon with the sale price and showed the final price so the shopper could decide if they wanted to add it to their list. We posted which coupon circular had the needed coupon, referencing the date the circular came out in the newspaper. Rather than cutting out coupons, shoppers could learn to simply write that Sunday's date on the front of the circular and save them all in a box or a file. When shoppers printed their selected shopping list from our website, they would cut out only the coupons needed for the selected deals, which would take ten to fifteen minutes per week instead of many hours. This process took more research and data entry time on our end but made it possible for shoppers to save dramatically with little effort. We called it the Coupon Mom System and it was our secret sauce. People loved it.

At the time a competing coupon website charged sixty dollars a month for a similar grocery-deal listing service, using the traditional coupon method that took shoppers hours a week. Our website was free to use and had this spiffy feature using the dated coupon circular that dramatically cut shoppers' time investment. Once CouponMom.com became well-known among coupon shoppers, the members of the sixty-dollar-a-month site complained to the owner and insisted their website add the feature that we had, which they did. Eventually, when hundreds of people started their own coupon websites after the 2008 recession, they all included our easy organizing feature, under their own name, as the industry standard.

HOW TO FIND YOUR IDEA

Just because someone else has already created a similar idea doesn't mean you can't come up with a better version. The sixty-dollar-a-month subscription site began one year before we started Coupon Mom. We could have easily said, "Oh, someone else is already doing that" and given up on our idea. The countless people who started coupon websites after us could have said the same thing. Instead, we were all able to help more people by providing multiple websites with more information. We all experienced the joy of helping others with our own style of teaching. When you step into the arena with your improved version, it may end up shaping the rest of the industry and even helping your competitors help more people too. That's how God's economy works. Crazy.

Identify an area of experience or interest.

What is a segment or category of business that you understand? Do you have a hobby you love? Are there problems you see that need solutions? Perhaps your big idea is a solution in an area you really enjoy, and you understand the existing problems to solve. Identifying a solution for people like you is the easiest route since you naturally understand the target market. Understanding and relating to your audience is critical for a successful product or service.

Years ago, a woman called me to discuss a website she created in the online coupon segment. She and her partner had received funding from investors. It had been nearly two years since they'd started their website and it was not gaining traction. The two founders were almost out of money and had spent two years living as frugally as possible. They approached me to buy the website.

She explained what they did for coupon shoppers, and we discussed it. Although the website looked professional and worked well technically, its service was of no practical use to a real coupon user. It gave users the ability to save the link for the printable coupon they liked, and when they were about to go shopping, they could print the coupon. What the founders of this website didn't understand was that each coupon had a maximum number of prints allocated by the advertiser and may be available for only a couple hours if it was popular. Waiting to print would likely cause the shopper to miss out altogether. This premise of saving links for convenience had no value.

This couple had started a coupon site because the industry was at its peak that year, but they were obviously not users themselves. They developed their idea in a vacuum and put big money and a lot of time into an impractical idea. When I explained why their premise wouldn't appeal to users, they suggested I buy the site and change its premise. That was an easy decision—no, thank you.

Ultimately they pivoted and changed the website to serve a different segment of the market, and I hope it became successful. It was a good example of why having money and brilliance isn't enough to guarantee a successful business. In fact, having a great idea and being willing to work at it can overcome a lack of money or even average intelligence. I had no extra money to put into a business, and I'm not ashamed to say I was a B student at a state university. In spite of that, our dream became a multimillion-dollar business that helped people, and I was doing something I loved. If you can find your good idea in your immediate area of interest or expertise, you'll be more likely to achieve your dream.

HAVING MONEY AND BRILLIANCE ISN'T ENOUGH TO GUARANTEE A SUCCESSFUL BUSINESS.

You may not want to pursue a big business idea. Becoming a billionaire may not be your dream. That's okay, because very few people become billionaires. But millions make a difference in the world, though they may never become famous or rich. It may be that money and fame weren't their objectives. Making a difference for something or someone was their reward.

Be a Rachel.

Years ago I presented the Cut Out Hunger idea for schools to use for food drives at a PTA meeting. Rachel, another presenter, had a heart for helping foster children. She was actually holding her foster baby on her hip during her entire presentation. She explained that the state provided foster families with a stipend for basic expenses for the children, but there was rarely extra money for nicer clothes, shoes, bicycles, backpacks, and other items that children at school had. In many cases the biological children in foster families had these items, but the foster children didn't. Rachel's dream was to collect good clothes, warm coats, new underwear, backpacks, bicycles, books, equipment, toys, and more to supply to foster families at no cost. She was collecting everything at her house and sorting items in her basement. Then families could come shop for what they needed without paying a dime.

Rachel's sincere love for foster children and her passion for helping them was obvious. She wasn't trying to be a polished speaker. She was just doing her best to get more donations so she could help more children. It must have taken her untold hours to promote her cause, collect and sort the items, and help the families as they shopped—all while taking care of a house full of foster children herself. That meeting was twenty years ago, and she is still one of the most inspiring people I've ever met.

Today Rachel has a nonprofit called the Foster Care Support Foundation in her hometown of Roswell, Georgia. Instead of sorting clothes in her basement, she now has a staff, warehouse space, a posse of volunteers, and strong financial support. We've sent her a check every year. She probably didn't realize twenty years ago how her genuine love for those children would touch the hearts of the people in the room. She was just hoping for a few donations.

When you land on your big idea, be a Rachel. Don't worry about impressing people with anything but genuine love for your project or cause. They will see your heart and will be drawn to support it. Rachel hasn't made a billion dollars, but the impact she has made in the lives of foster families, foster children, and her supporters is priceless.

> **DON'T WORRY ABOUT IMPRESSING PEOPLE WITH ANYTHING BUT GENUINE LOVE FOR YOUR PROJECT OR CAUSE.**

Ask yourself fun questions.

What did you want to be as a child? When people asked you what you were going to be when you grew up, what did you say? We can be many different things in our lives; you don't have to settle for what you have called yourself for years. You may be a young mother, you may be a retiree, you may be a college graduate with a brand-new degree and no idea of what the future holds yet.

I was a waitress, then a salesperson, then a stay-at-home mom, then a grocery coupon expert (you can make up anything, you know), and now I am an author. I am old enough to be a retiree, but I don't really like that title. It makes it seem like there's not much left in life. And you know what I wanted to be when I was a child? An author. That's what I always dreamed of: living on a farm and writing in a peaceful room with a view of the countryside. I don't live on a farm, but that's okay. The important thing is that there's still time in this beautiful life to try new things.

Try telling yourself who you want to be.

I went to my first writer's workshop a few years ago and the instructor said to me, "You are an author and a speaker." I nodded. Then he said, "Say it out loud. Say that you are an author and a speaker." So I said it out loud, and you know what? It felt true. Even though it hadn't happened yet, just saying that out loud started the process of becoming something new. As soon as you say it, you'll be on your way to becoming who you aspire to be.

WHAT I LEARNED

Write down a sentence or two that describes your general dream. Once you have that running around in your mind all the time, as you go through daily life you'll start noticing problems, opportunities, and solutions that could become your big idea. Think about it, pray about it, and pay attention. Your lightbulb moment may be just around the corner.

Keep it to yourself in the beginning. Once you have landed on your big idea, keep it to yourself like Sara Blakely did. Not only will you avoid people's natural tendency to play devil's advocate and point out why you shouldn't be wasting your time and money on that idea, but it will avoid putting a strain on your relationships. Another reason to keep a lid on your idea is that you may want to get it established before someone agrees that it's a great idea and they beat you to market. You never know.

Don't create your idea in a vacuum. You may think you have a solution to a problem you observe, but remember that we don't know what we don't know. If your idea is for a consumer segment you are not experienced in, try to find people who are consumers for that type of product or service and get their input. You can ask questions or do polls on social media platforms or simply ask people you know to test it. A lot of time and money could have been saved by the couple who tried to sell me their website if they'd floated their idea by real coupon users first.

Affirm to yourself who you want to be or what you want to do. Tell yourself that you already are that person. Keep saying it over and over. Continue telling yourself who you want to be, and you'll move in that direction.

Rejection: Recalculating Your Route

No one likes to be told no, so give yourself a minute to breathe and process it. Then, turn the no into an "I can." Start to think of a new plan—find a different door, and if you can't find a door, look for a window.

—BOBBI BROWN, FOUNDER OF JONES ROAD BEAUTY

W hat do you know about the hunger cause?" the director of a large nonprofit serving low-income clients demanded. "It's not practical to think grocery coupons could help our clients."

When we started the Cut Out Hunger website, my focus was to find a coupon company, grocery store chain, or hunger organization to take the idea over. After all, we didn't have the money or staff to grow the concept, and time was of the essence. Children were going hungry every day, and people needed to learn how to get free groceries as soon as possible. A big organization with plenty of staff and money could quickly get the idea off the ground.

Our church's minister was supportive and helpful from the beginning. He arranged a meeting with the director of a large nonprofit so I could get feedback on my idea. My website listed the best coupon deals each week, and I thought the organization could publicize the free website to their low-income clients to help them stretch their grocery dollars. The director had been a leader of the poverty cause in our state for twenty-five years and was passionate about helping the less fortunate. So of course he would love the idea! He would probably adopt it as an official program and ask me to be his volunteer staff member to run it. When he endorsed it, the national office would naturally want to expand the idea, and it would spread across the country like wildfire. Food donations would be pouring into food banks in every city. The White House would probably give me a humanitarian award for the brilliant idea. The possibilities were endless.

EMBARRASSMENT INSTEAD OF AMAZEMENT

A church member offered to join me since she knew the director personally, and we drove to the meeting together. It was like going to meet the Wizard of Oz. He could snap his fingers and make this incredible idea a huge, national success overnight. My PowerPoint presentation was locked and loaded. Have you ever been so sure of something that you couldn't imagine how it could go wrong? Have you ever been so excited to share something, knowing that people would be impressed by your creativity or initiative?

Just three sentences into the presentation, when I was

not even past the first slide, the director interrupted. He was visibly angry. He launched into explaining how he'd been a leader in fighting poverty for decades and understood the issue better than anyone. Someone who had just discovered their local food pantry a few months earlier couldn't possibly under-

HAVE YOU EVER BEEN SO SURE OF SOMETHING THAT YOU COULDN'T IMAGINE HOW IT COULD GO WRONG?

stand the complexities of the issue. The idea of teaching low-income people to buy food with coupons was naive. Struggling families didn't have money to buy the newspaper for coupons, they didn't have computers to use a website, and they didn't even have transportation to drive to a grocery store. Many of them lived in neighborhoods without grocery stores at all. Besides that, he was the one who had relationships with the coupon companies and grocery store chains. They were his largest financial supporters, after all. I didn't need to be meeting with them to enlist their support of my idea. It was clear that he wasn't interested in getting to slide two of the presentation!

He also said that teaching people how to buy their own food with coupons would make them dependent on the coupons. Pretty soon too many people would be using them, and the food companies would stop issuing them. Then what would those people we had made dependent on coupons do? Our efforts to teach how to use coupons would hurt the very ones we were trying to help. (By the way, this rationale is ridiculous and turned out to be wrong. But back to the story.)

We ended the meeting and thanked the director for his time. He said it would be okay for us to buy food for charity with coupons, but we shouldn't try to spread this message. He actually granted me permission to donate food to charity! The meeting ended in embarrassment, certainly not in amazement at my brilliance.

We drove home in silence and disappointment. But by the end of that thirty-minute drive, I started to feel like he was wrong. Who needs permission to donate food to charity or permission to teach others how to donate food to charity? Who needs permission to share my idea with companies invested in the ideas of increasing coupon usage and grocery sales? Wouldn't anyone who was fighting a social problem welcome the help of like-minded people?

The director's rejection reinforced our belief in the idea. No single person has the power to determine the success or failure of our ideas. The charity director might not have liked the concept, but God had plans for it anyway. Perhaps this is how God works. When a door closes on an idea we have, it forces us to lean on Him and trust that there is a better path. Can you recall rejection experiences in your life that were discouraging but ended up being the best turn in your life path at the time? Perhaps you've experienced disappointment recently, but you haven't had enough time to see God's lesson. Remember, the story isn't over yet. There's something better ahead that will explain the reason for the disappointment, and you may end up being thankful it happened.

As it turned out, what happened for us was far better than what that nonprofit could have provided. God had a much better path, even if we didn't realize it at the time. When you are passionate about your idea, you are its best ambassador, so you don't have to recruit anyone else for the role. You can ask like-minded people if they want to be part of it, but you don't need the blessing of ordinary mortals to justify the validity of your idea.

> **WHEN YOU ARE PASSIONATE ABOUT YOUR IDEA, YOU ARE ITS BEST AMBASSADOR.**

The leader we met with had an organization that did wonderful work, *and* our idea also had great potential. It wasn't either/or. There's always plenty of room to support an important cause—in fact, the more, the better. We could each do God's work in our own way. The harvest is plentiful but the workers are few (Matthew 9:37), so let's not push any away. And let's be nice to each other.

YOUR WORTH VERSUS OTHERS' OPINIONS

Not everyone will like your idea or see its potential. Although it's helpful to have supporters, don't be discouraged if you get a *no, thank you* when you approach those you expect to be interested. Everyone has their own ideas and challenges, and they may not have the energy or resources to help with your new idea. Don't take a no too personally. There's lots going on in others' situations that we aren't aware of, and those things usually have nothing to do with us.

When you approach a potential supporter, it's always wise to do your homework. Spend time understanding what their major projects, issues, and challenges may be. Practical issues like funding and measurement are critical in the nonprofit world, just as they are in the private sector. We can incorrectly assume that anyone who cares about the same social issue would naturally want to work together. In general, that makes sense. But the reality is that every organization has resource challenges. The gentleman we approached had many wonderful projects competing for limited resources, and we had an untested idea that couldn't be measured at that time. Financial sponsors appreciate tangible results and data showing the value of their donations; he needed projects with measurable results. So it makes sense that he didn't embrace the idea.

Perhaps he and I were too much alike. We each liked to start new ideas, we liked to lead the charge, and we liked to be the one giving the presentation. There's nothing wrong with any of those things, but they can create the potential for a clash. God gave each of us our ideas and our visions, and the gentleman and I were both successful in our own versions of helping the hunger cause. But we should build each other's ideas up, not tear them down. We probably had a lot more in common than my ego could see, and with a little humility we could have recognized that and become friends.

It's encouraging when we read stories about people we respect and how they overcame rejections. Let's learn from them and skip right over our next rejection, choosing to believe it's a blip and not a defining moment. For example, Meryl Streep is described as the best actress of her generation.[1] She is known for being able to play a wide variety of characters with award-winning performances every time. Her talent is a gift to the world.

Early in her career Meryl tried out for the lead part in the movie *King Kong*. She met the producer, and he asked his son in Italian so she wouldn't understand, "Why did you bring this ugly thing?" Apparently Meryl knew Italian, because she replied, "Sorry that I am not beautiful enough to star in *King Kong*."[2] Fortunately, she had enough confidence in her talent to skip right over that rejection, which led to many wonderful performances that we've been able to enjoy for years. She has won three Academy Awards, eight Golden Globe Awards, and several prestigious honorary awards. Perhaps being rejected to star in *King Kong* was for the best.[3]

It's your vision. If you can see it, don't let anyone rain on your parade. And you don't need to rain on anyone else's parade to be successful. If you believe in your idea and believe that God does too, keep moving. Look for another door. You have a gift for the world; it's your responsibility and privilege to get it out there. You may have to do it yourself, and that's okay, because you're the best one to do it. God picked you. He believes in you, and that's more than enough to get you to your dream.

WHAT I LEARNED

Don't expect one person to be a savior. Many people will contribute to your journey in some way. One person isn't likely to flip a switch and get you from zero to one hundred overnight. Look for supporters and partners with mutual interests, but if they aren't interested, move on. There are millions of people who may want to help you. Most important, it's your work that will keep your cause moving forward—not a single person or event somehow magically getting you to the finish line.

Don't take rejection of your idea personally. It's easy to feel personally rejected when someone turns down our proposal, because we are so emotionally invested. Remember, they aren't rejecting you; they might not even know you. Just because your idea isn't right for their company or organization does not mean it's a bad idea. Don't let small rejections derail your enthusiasm. Keep looking for new doors.

Don't waste energy making someone a villain. It's a natural defense mechanism to view the person who rejected your idea as a bad guy. You may realize later that their rejection was actually a blessing in disguise because the alternate path was much better for you. Rather than making the person a villain, see them as another one of God's children pursuing their own dream for loving and helping others. Remember that everyone has their own ideas, dreams, and vision. Sometimes we fit together, and sometimes we have separate paths working toward the same goal. There's plenty of room for everyone to be successful.

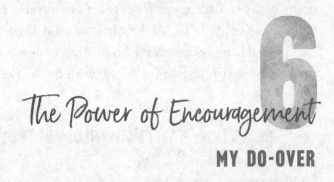

The Power of Encouragement

MY DO-OVER

> Let us consider how we may spur one
> another on toward love and good deeds.
>
> —HEBREWS 10:24

J. T. Harding left home at the age of seventeen to pursue a career in the music industry. In his memoir, *Party Like a Rockstar*, J. T. shared countless stories of having the songs he'd written rejected by music producers. He claims his heart has been broken more times than the McDonald's ice cream machine! But he never let rejections stop him from continuing to write songs and pitch them to producers.

J. T. pitched one song continually for over three years until it was finally produced—perhaps you've heard of the song "Smile" by Uncle Kracker? It was Uncle Kracker's biggest hit, went multiplatinum, and stormed the pop and country charts. Thirty years after leaving home, J. T. is one of the most successful songwriters in Nashville. He has written many of my favorite songs from great artists including Kenny Chesney, Keith Urban, Blake Shelton, and Darius Rucker. Millions of listeners are thankful he didn't let rejection get in the way of sharing beautiful music with the world.[1]

REJECTION MAY LEAD TO OPPORTUNITY

Sometimes a slammed door may be God's guardrail to protect us from our own limited plan. He may have something better in mind that requires Him to block a path. That's how it happened for me. A few weeks after the very humbling rejection experience with the director of the large nonprofit, another opportunity came up. The director of our local food pantry, North Fulton Community Charities, was willing to hear our pitch. This was the small food pantry where we took our food donations. They had only three full-time employees, which included the director, and they relied on volunteers for almost all their staffing. About one hundred families a day came for food, so they had their hands full. They certainly weren't in a position to take over our idea.

Everyone in our community respected Barbara Duffy, the executive director.

> SOMETIMES A SLAMMED DOOR MAY BE GOD'S GUARDRAIL TO PROTECT US FROM OUR OWN LIMITED PLAN.

Hundreds of civic organizations and places of worship in our zip code supported this food pantry. Several people at our church volunteered there, and our minister said Barbara would probably be a receptive audience to my idea. We'd been taking food almost every day for a couple of months, but Barbara was so busy seeing clients, I still hadn't met her. My minister set up an appointment with her, and I went with the same PowerPoint presentation.

I headed into this meeting with cautious optimism instead of the brazen, assumptive attitude of last time. It wouldn't hurt to be humbler about my idea. Being seriously humbled is very effective at making us even more humble!

Barbara was friendly and kind. She politely listened to me present every single slide of the PowerPoint, including the graph that showed we'd donated $1,400 worth of groceries at an 85 percent discount over a two-month period—just by using coupons. She nodded throughout and occasionally laughed out loud. The final line of the presentation was, "Would you feel comfortable promoting this website to your charity's supporters?"

She looked up and said, "I don't understand this coupon thing at all. But if anyone ever comes into my office with a PowerPoint presentation for an idea to feed the hungry, the answer is *yes*!" It was the best moment, one I still replay in my mind and share. Just a few words of sincere encouragement can make all the difference in making a person's dream a reality. Let's remember that.

Barbara called her assistant director into her office and scheduled a presentation at their volunteer luncheon the next week. She wrote an article about the website in the charity's newsletter, which was sent to thousands of supporters, and contacted the community newspaper to do an interview and article about the program, which led to more coverage throughout our city. She put the word out to leaders of religious and civic organizations who needed speakers, which opened doors for me to speak to dozens of groups about Cut Out Hunger over the next few years. Her volunteers took the idea to their neighborhoods. Barbara lit the match that spread the word, and it took off in our local area.

Most important, she provided affirmation and encouragement, which was empowering. Her response and follow-up actions encouraged me beyond words. It was the perfect timing. For the past twenty years I've enjoyed a special relationship with North Fulton Community Charities in many ways—from being a donor to a volunteer to a board member. When Coupon Mom first started making money, writing the first big check to their charity was so exciting and emotional. Barbara said she was excited when she got it! There really are no words for how much her support and encouragement meant, especially on the heels of such a harsh rejection. The entire experience with both directors demonstrated that our worst no could actually be God's best yes.

THE BENEFITS OF HUMBLE SERVICE

We can move mountains when we encourage ideas. Even when we aren't the ones directly responsible for an initiative that helps others, when we look up and say, "The answer is *yes*" at every wise opportunity, we become key players in

God's plan to help people help others. Barbara was in the habit of encouraging people at all income levels. She encouraged the charity's clients who had nowhere to turn when the electric company turned off their power, and she encouraged wealthier people who discovered that money didn't fulfill them as they'd expected. Her charity encouraged clients, volunteers, donors, board members, and anyone who walked through her door who needed help or who wanted to help. She said yes to anyone looking for encouragement, fulfillment, or both. Let's be like Barbara.

Being humbled by the earlier nonprofit director also forced me to recognize my impatience. When we're impatient, we are telling God that His timing isn't good enough for us. But when we are humbled, we lower our expectations and we become more patient. When we are humbled, we are happier with smaller successes over a longer period of time. Being more patient allows God's timing to do its work. Working with the smaller food pantry felt like a very big deal after being rejected by the large one. And it turned out that the smaller food pantry was able to move mountains after all.

Our personalities can also impact who we are most likely to link elbows with as we go along the path to our dream. Barbara's personality was very different from the other director's. Barbara did not care for the limelight and was never trying to get the spotlight on herself. She worked alongside the other employees to meet with clients, worked in the food pantry, and got the newsletter typed up and mailed, among many other tasks. She is one of the humblest people you'd ever meet, with a huge heart for helping people in need. Over the thirty-five years she's been the charity's director, it's grown in staffing, seen financial donations increase, and moved to a larger building. When people complimented her for her leadership in growing the organization, she'd say, "This is not the type of organization that we want to grow. It shows that the problem is getting worse. Ideally, we'd like to solve the problem so that we'd be out of business."

When we spoke recently about our first meeting with my PowerPoint, she said, "Well of course I liked the idea! It was fully developed and ready to go. We needed all the help we could get!" Barbara personified humility and service to the people in our community who needed assistance. And it was clear that her service filled her with joy. Not because of accolades or public approval, but because she personally connected with the clients and supporters and knew she was making a difference in their lives. Barbara was in the business of encouraging people, loving them, and building them up every day.

That's how love is. When we freely give it to those who are most overlooked instead of seeking approval for ourselves, we are the ones who are filled with joy. Joy is God's reminder that we're on the right path. We don't need titles or accolades from people to know we are doing God's work. We'll just know.

> **JOY IS GOD'S REMINDER THAT WE'RE ON THE RIGHT PATH.**

Barbara was a fun, optimistic supporter of our cause from the beginning. In the early years, a small publisher published my first book. It taught the reader everything about strategic shopping, coupons, and donating free food to charity. Unfortunately, the publisher printed far more books than they could sell and ended up with a warehouse full of books. I felt terrible that the publisher had lost money betting on me. Rather than throwing the books away, they offered to sell the entire inventory to me for a dollar a copy. This was great for us because it was much less expensive than publishing marketing materials would be, and it was far more helpful in teaching our message. It also helped the publisher make their money back, which made me feel better.

We used the book to raise money for North Fulton Community Charities. The first time we tried this, I felt a little sheepish promoting a book and didn't expect many sales. At the end of a Rotary Club breakfast talk, I held up a copy of my book and explained that they were available for twenty dollars each, with 100 percent of the proceeds going to North Fulton Community Charities. One of the members immediately walked up to the podium, grabbed the book, and traded it for a twenty-dollar bill. Then he looked at the group and said, "Okay, everyone—get in line. We are buying all her books." And they did. It was so overwhelming and exciting. I drove to Barbara's office, told her what had happened, and dumped a pile of twenties on her desk, over $800. We couldn't believe it. It was so fun to share the joy of all that was happening with her.

We continued to take this approach with speaking engagements. It always worked, and we ended up being able to give thousands of dollars to the charity while educating people on how to be strategic shoppers and food pantry donors.

It's all about perspective—the world's view or God's view. We could either look at that first book as a commercial failure in the publishing world because it sold so few copies, or we could see it as the unexpected gift it was—a marketing and fundraising success for the charity we loved. That's how God's economy works; it doesn't follow the same success metrics as the world's. Sometimes it takes a pile of twenty-dollar bills and a big laugh to remind us that God has our back, all the time.

SUCCESS DOESN'T HAVE TO CHANGE YOU

Over the next several years, many media requests and business opportunities came in, including a new book deal, a product line of Coupon Mom coupon organizers, spokesperson deals, and interviews on other media outlets. It was exciting. Of course, I called Barbara to report all this craziness. She was one of the few people who could understand the magnitude of this dream coming true. We laughed together, because she knew the obstacles that had been thrown in my way, and she knew how much her encouragement had meant to me. We shared in the joy and wonder of this beautiful road God was leading us on. As you face challenges along the way, find friends to share the success and joy of your efforts, because it is a lot more fun than going it alone.

> **FIND FRIENDS TO SHARE THE SUCCESS AND JOY OF YOUR EFFORTS.**

At the height of CouponMom.com's popularity, our city's newspaper did a profile on the website. They interviewed Barbara and asked her what I was like. She said, "Her success hasn't changed her a bit. She is the same down-to-earth person she always was."[2]

How would I have changed? We usually don't know how to be something different than we are, and when we try to be something different, we usually do a bad job of it. At the age of forty-five—my age then—most of us are fully baked. It's like that old saying, "Be yourself. Everyone else is taken." That applies to both ends of the spectrum—at the beginning when you need more confidence, and further along the path when you experience success and need a little humility. No matter what happens, remember who you are. You are the special person God created you to be, and that's constant. Plus, it's the easiest way to be.

Many years later, we staged a Coupon Mom Olympics event at our local grocery store. It was a great way to get media coverage for North Fulton Community Charities while raising food donations. The challenge was for coupon shoppers to compete against each other to see who could buy the most groceries for the charity at the lowest cost using coupons and the fifty dollars we gave each of them. We hung a big Coupon Mom Olympics banner over the checkout lane.

On the day of the event, two TV news teams came to interview Barbara and me. The shoppers did an impressive job getting hundreds of dollars of groceries for fifty dollars each. We carefully calculated shoppers' scores, and the winner won by pennies. All the contestants received free gift-card prizes from the store, and we had lunch together afterward. Barbara was able to talk about all the services North Fulton Community Charities provided to the community on the news. The event was another reminder that God wants us to show His love by helping others, and that we can have fun doing it. God's work isn't really work at all when it fills us with joy.

In reflecting back on that time, I can see that it's a blessing that the first nonprofit director didn't accept our idea. It wasn't right for that organization, and that rejection led to Barbara. As a result, raising food donations for North Fulton Community Charities by working with dozens of civic organizations and religious groups was fulfilling and fun work. We developed friendships with other donors, staff members, board members, and volunteers. Today I cherish volunteering in that same food pantry to fill clients' orders, hear their stories, and try to provide encouragement to them. We don't need to be endorsed by a charity or leader of a cause to succeed—we just need to love the organization or the mission.

WHAT I LEARNED

God wants us to encourage and build each other up. We don't always have to be the ones with the ideas or the ones getting the accolades. Paying attention and being open to others' ideas gives us the opportunity to lift them up and remind them they are responding to God's call for their life. Encouragement gives others the confidence they need to move ahead with their dreams. That's a gift that costs us nothing and may be priceless to the one you are encouraging. And ultimately you will share in their joy.

Being humbled develops patience. Experiencing rejection of your big idea can be humbling but also helps you develop patience. Success cannot be reached overnight, and every step in the process helps us grow in wisdom and maturity. You know your idea is valid and important, but the people who don't agree with you are not the ones to trust with its growth. Move on and be patient. You will find supporters in time, and becoming more patient will help you in countless ways as you pursue your dream.

Giving back fulfills us. As people encourage you along your path to your dream, you may be in a position in the future to support and encourage them in their dream. And in God's economy, you can't outgive God. Whenever we give back to someone or something, we are the ones who end up receiving the most. Encouragement multiplies itself when we give it back and forth to each other.

7

Just Ten Minutes

DISCOVER PIVOTAL PEOPLE

This is great, you should definitely
get it on national television!
I know the producer at *Good Morning America* . . .

—DAVID GREGG

After consumer adviser Clark Howard recommended my website on his radio show in November 2003, it took just one call to get booked on *Good Day Atlanta*, a live morning news show that aired daily. The producer booked a segment in December for me to demonstrate how to buy food for charity with coupons, since December is the busiest month of the year for food drives.

David Gregg was the other guest appearing in the same half-hour time slot, so we waited together backstage. It was very early in the morning. We shouldn't expect anyone to be friendly and chatty at that hour. Fortunately, David was very friendly and chatty. A television professional specializing in electronics, he traveled around the country appearing on local and national TV to give advice on the best products to buy.

David did his segment, there was a commercial, and then it was my turn. We had a table full of grocery items purchased at no cost with coupons, and they were all good for charity. In spite of my being a little nervous, the segment went well. Doing it was no different than presentations to local groups, and I'd done plenty of those.

David was polite and seemed interested in how our system worked to get free groceries every week. Afterward he said, "Okay, I was going to wait until I saw you do your segment before I said anything. This is great—you should definitely get it on national television." I laughed, because I'd sent emails to all the national morning shows multiple times with no response. How did someone get on national TV?

Then he made that fateful statement that changed everything for us. "I know the producer at *Good Morning America* who decides which guests go on their show. Her name is Lisa, and she answers her own phone. Call her on Friday after two o'clock and tell her what you've got in thirty seconds or less. And don't tell her that I gave you her name." He shared Lisa's full name with instructions to call the ABC switchboard and ask for her. It was that easy.

The next day I called Lisa right at two o'clock. She answered her phone, and that started the thirty-second pitch. We had a program that made it easy for people to get free groceries with coupons that worked every week, in every city. The program was free to users. She said, "That's interesting. Send me some information and your contact information." That was it.

YOU CAN'T REACH YOUR GOALS ALONE

We didn't hear from Lisa immediately. Over the next few months, I sent updates whenever we had local media coverage or added an improvement to the website. The frequent contacts may have been obnoxious, but she was our ticket to reaching a very large audience in one appearance. What did we have to lose?

Back then TV stations were only beginning to put videos of news stories on their websites. A few months after first talking to Lisa, our local news did a shopping segment with me, showing incredible savings at the grocery store. It was professionally filmed and edited, and they put that video on the station's website. I was able to send an email with a link to the news story to Lisa. That did it. She saw the program in action, and she decided to invite me to demonstrate it on their show. A few weeks later I was on my way to New York for my first segment on *GMA*.

I called David immediately. He was excited too. Without his help, it wouldn't have happened. He'd become a participant in our vision simply by being generous with his information. It didn't cost him anything, but his contribution was

> YOU CAN'T REACH YOUR BOLD VISION BY YOURSELF.

invaluable and changed the path of our dream overnight. Ultimately, his generosity helped millions of people save money for their families.

Throughout the twenty-year Coupon Mom journey, David was one of countless people who contributed to the effort in some way. Without them, this unbelievable story would not have been possible. You can't reach your bold vision by yourself.

There were a few people who were absolutely critical to its success. In fact, without them, the website probably wouldn't have grown beyond our suburb. Instead we reached millions of people, which was our dream. When I think about how they all entered the Coupon Mom journey, I can see how it would have been easy to miss out on connecting with them. By taking just a few extra minutes to get to know them, our dreams can take an entirely new trajectory.

That said, if those people hadn't been generous with just a few minutes of their time to talk to me, we would have missed out entirely on their contribution. In just a few moments of conversation our lives can intersect with someone else's in a meaningful way. Ten minutes of genuine conversation can open doors that can lead to something remarkable. Can you think of people you've discovered by spending a few minutes taking an interest in them beyond just polite introductions? People who became good friends, business colleagues, or perhaps even a spouse?

David's willingness to share his connections took our path in a completely new direction. In reflecting on this time, it seems God wasn't asking me to give up my drive toward our purpose. He just had a better map to use that reached our purpose much more effectively. It's our *purpose* that God wants us to hold tightly, not our *plans*. He has gifted us with skills and abilities like drive, energy, and the willingness to do the necessary work. God wasn't asking me to give up my drive. He was showing me *where* to drive—to accomplish His purposes for our vision.

> **IT'S OUR *PURPOSE* THAT GOD WANTS US TO HOLD TIGHTLY, NOT OUR *PLANS*.**

PERSISTENCE LEADS TO PIVOTAL CONNECTIONS

Have you ever felt that God was giving you a hand, an open door, just when you needed it? Based on the timing alone, have you ever felt like the only way it could have happened was if God had helped you out? We need to get on our knees and ask God for His direction, and when He gives us direction, we need to get up off our knees and follow His lead. Even if it seems radically different from our original plans.

Think about the what-ifs. What if David hadn't been there the same day I was? *Good Day Atlanta* was a daily show, and he traveled all over the country for his appearances. I was there one day. What if he had been scheduled in a different half hour of the show? We wouldn't have been standing backstage together. What if David had had something else on his mind and didn't feel like chatting? What if he'd wanted to protect his media contacts and wouldn't share them with a stranger? If it weren't for meeting David that day, *Good Morning America* would not have gifted me with the Coupon Mom brand, which launched our program nationally and opened up countless doors for our cause.

Have you ever met a pivotal person like David? Has anyone ever had the grace and generosity to give you information or provide a connection that changed everything for your vision? Or have you ever been a pivotal person like David? We have probably all had the opportunity to be on the giving side of helpful information and will have many more opportunities in the future to make a difference in this easy way. So let's pay attention and be interested. You'll never know what you can contribute to someone else's vision and how the domino effect could help more people—maybe even millions of people—in just ten minutes of your time.

Lisa called our home the night of that first *GMA* segment and left a message on our voice mail. Her first sentence was, "Thank you for your persistence." Most people wouldn't have been as persistent, because politeness generally dictates behavior. Who knows what the politeness limit is on emails and phone calls, but I bet I had exceeded it. My obsessive drive, the one I'd asked God to take away, propelled me to continue sending her email updates and voice mail messages. Fortunately, she did not ignore them. She took the bold and risky step of putting an amateur on her national news show. Her decision to do that changed everything, and I will forever be grateful to David for sharing Lisa's name with me, and to Lisa for using her creativity and influence to give Coupon Mom a platform on *GMA*.

WHAT I LEARNED

Talk to everyone, even if it is 7 a.m. You never know where a conversation will lead. If the other person isn't interested in chatting, you'll be able to tell right away and can be quiet. But if you don't initiate conversation, you may miss a big opportunity.

Be sincerely interested in others. Once you're having a conversation, really pay attention and listen. People open up when they feel the other person is genuinely interested, and we can tell when someone is faking interest. And people are interesting, so make it a fun experience to get to know them, even in a short conversation.

Exchange contact information, if appropriate. Don't be afraid to offer a way to contact each other if you've made an interesting connection. Offer to send them helpful information or a contact name of someone they may like to connect with. Information costs nothing to give and can be life-changing for someone else.

Show your appreciation. Be sure to go back to the person who offered you information to let them know it went well (if it did) and how much you appreciated their support. Thanking them allows them to be a participant in the success of your journey and lets them have the satisfaction of knowing that they helped make a difference in many people's lives.

Pivotal People

NANETTE

> I planted the seed, Apollos watered it, but God has
> been making it grow . . . The one who plants and
> the one who waters have one purpose, and they will
> each be rewarded according to their own labor.

> —1 CORINTHIANS 3:6, 8

When I picked up David Gregg's phone call several years after we'd met, he led with, "I haven't seen you on TV in a while. What's going on?"

After the *Good Morning America* contract ended at the beginning of 2007, our website was earning enough money to support our family. My husband offered to take a leave of absence from his career to manage our home and our kids' lives so I could focus on learning more about the business side of running a website. Everything was going well.

So when David called, I explained that my *GMA*

relationship had run its course, but that was fine. Anyone would be lucky to be on their show once, much less seventeen times. It was a great experience, but being a long-term television savings expert wasn't in the cards. Even a New York publicist I'd hired recently wasn't able to book me on other news shows. It was clear that we had exhausted the coupon subject.

David wouldn't accept that explanation. He said, "No! You need to get back on TV. You just need a better publicist. I have the perfect one for you—my publicist, Nanette. You *need* Nanette. Call her immediately." Once again, he generously provided guidance and helpful information. And his generosity changed everything—even more than being on *GMA* had.

ENTER NANETTE

The next step was calling Nanette in January 2008. We had an enjoyable conversation and hit it off immediately. Nanette was sweet, kind, optimistic, and calm. She was originally from a small town in Tennessee and had spent the first ten years of her career working as a producer at the *Today* show in New York. Then she moved back home to Tennessee, married her high school prom date, and started a business handling media relations for "not famous" people like me—authors and topic experts. She was selective about who she accepted because she needed to believe in the person's topic and their cause, and she wanted topics that news shows would welcome. Later Nanette told me that she felt God had put the two of us together at the perfect time. She loved the idea of helping people save money and feed the hungry.

At the time we had no idea what that phone call would set in motion. The first step was to see if the grocery coupon topic still had legs, so our goal was to get on national television one more time. She thought that was possible but said, "Do not ask me to get you on *Oprah*. That is the first thing everyone asks their publicist, and it is the number one pet peeve of every publicist I know." I assured her I wouldn't ask her to do that. It would be wonderful if any national news show would book us.

Nanette was more than just an excellent publicist. She was one of the best people you'd ever know. Everyone who knew her loved her. Over the years she was like a best friend, a sister, a mother, an adviser, and a coach all rolled into one. She had countless friends, and it wouldn't be surprising if we all thought we were her best friend. Nanette made everyone feel special.

Some people act one way on Sundays at church and another way during the week, or they act one way in their personal life and another way at work. Nanette was the same in every situation. She was the most loving, caring person and a friend to everyone she encountered. A faithful believer in God, she lived her faith every day in the way she loved and treated everyone—whether they were friends, family, or business colleagues. Nanette must have really stood out in the New York television world where she worked for ten years. As a result, she had countless trusted friends in the business, which meant she had golden contacts. That's why she was selective about the clients she accepted. She would be asking her friends who worked as producers across several TV shows if they would have her clients on their shows. It was a huge gift that she would take me on as a client.

Over the next seven years of our working together, Nanette's efforts would dramatically grow our business, help millions of families, and even transform the coupon industry. On top of that, our business relationship became a genuine friendship, and she modeled what it really looked like to be a follower of Christ.

Nanette had a gift of encouraging people. She didn't tell people what to do; she told them who they were, and that made it easier for her clients to do a good job. From the beginning she would tell me, "You are the country's leading expert on grocery coupons." And that's what she told the TV producers she pitched to have me on their shows. Nanette's confidence in my abilities made me a better and more knowledgeable expert. When we show people that we believe in them, they may become even better versions of themselves.

> **WHEN WE SHOW PEOPLE THAT WE BELIEVE IN THEM, THEY MAY BECOME EVEN BETTER VERSIONS OF THEMSELVES.**

Let's talk about this for a minute. Most people are capable of using grocery coupons. Plenty use them too. Calling yourself the leading expert on using grocery coupons is like calling yourself the leading expert on eating ice cream. It's not rocket science, and most people could do it if they tried.

But somehow Nanette's confidence in my ability translated into confidence on the air. She made it easier to relax and have good discussions with the news anchors and reporters, as if we were just sitting around the kitchen table. Many of those reporters became my good friends over the years.

BELIEVING IN OTHERS

What if we did that with the people we love? Instead of telling them what to do or how to be, we could be telling them who we believe they are, or who we see them becoming. Then they could relax and see themselves in the same light. When the people we love tell us how they see us, we begin to believe it, and then we become more capable of what God wants us to do.

What if we were to listen to God more? What if we believed Him when He told us we are His dearly loved children, and that He created each of us with unique qualities to be the people He knows we can be? How would that change the way we see ourselves? How would that change our love for others? It would change everything.

The timing was perfect for me to land within Nanette's orbit. We didn't know that it was the beginning of a recession and that many TV news shows would want to feature savings topics like grocery coupons. Nanette said we were the perfect team because she had the contacts, and my media experience earned the producers' trust quickly. Her authentic, personal relationships in the TV world opened doors no one else had been able to open for me.

Nanette booked a segment on the *Today* show immediately. It was fun, it went well, and the viewers responded enthusiastically. Over time we had five *Today* show segments, and there were always interesting guests to chat with in the green room. By the way, Sara Blakely was there one day, and she is just as nice as she is successful. Meeting her was a thrill. She is the rock star of ordinary people pursuing their ideas to do extraordinary things. And any woman who has Spanx in her drawer would agree that she made an extraordinary contribution to this world!

In just the year 2008 Nanette booked sixteen national TV appearances across many networks, sometimes more than one a day. It all came so easily—we felt like we had landed on a path God had paved for us. We felt we were spreading a message that was really helping people.

Nanette's work helped make my dream come true— and she made the whole thing *fun*. Over our seven years of working together, she booked a total of thirty-eight national TV appearances and hundreds of local TV, radio, and print interviews. We joked that we were spreading the gospel of grocery coupons. Nanette's favorite quote was when Michelle Singletary of the *Washington Post* referred to me as "the rock star of the recession" in her column "The Color of Money." That always made her giggle. Millions of people used the website, told us stories of how their savings helped their families, and more than 80 percent said they donated food to charity. Ten percent of the website's members were on food stamps, so it really was helping people in the greatest financial need help themselves.

The overwhelming gratitude of the site's users was the

best part of the whole thing. We received many emails, but an unforgettable one was, "Thank you for your website. I'm saving so much money! My husband says that if I keep saving this much money, he's going to take me to Red Lobster for dinner!" There's so much to unpack there—but the bottom line is that not only was this helping her save money but it was also apparently helping her marriage! Emails like that reminded us that there were real people on the other side of this website, and it mattered to them. And isn't that how love works? When we give, when we try to help others, they end up filling us up with their gratitude and joy. The circle goes on. We just can't outgive God.

> WHEN WE GIVE, WHEN WE TRY TO HELP OTHERS, THEY END UP FILLING US UP WITH THEIR GRATITUDE AND JOY.

Nanette's optimism, encouragement, and coaching made me braver. She always referred to us as a team. We were friends having fun together. In 2008 when the media requests were coming in so fast that we had to juggle appearances, she said, "We are hot, hot, hot!" followed by her infectious laughter. She made the whole thing a fun adventure.

Have you ever had someone come alongside you who made you feel more capable? Someone who could see you differently than you saw yourself, and as a result, your perception of yourself changed? That's who a true encourager is. Someone who can help us see ourselves differently, in a better light. Having an encourager by your side can be the difference between a dream and reality.

And as encouragers, we can help someone else's dream come to fruition. When we encourage others in their vision, we become a part of their vision too. We can genuinely share in their happiness, simply because we took time to love them by letting them know who we believe they really are and what we believe they can accomplish. Sincere words of encouragement are powerful, and we can give them away at no cost.

Nanette and I talked on the phone several times a week for over seven years and had many laughs. Our relationship was much more than a business transaction. We prayed for each other through all kinds of life situations. We had our faith in common, and in the midst of all of it, we both believed that God had put us together at the right time. Nanette always credited God.

When we had our first conversation in 2008 about working together, the website had reached our original goal of 200,000 members. Seven years later we hit 7.5 million members—and millions of people used other coupon blogs similar to our site.

REMEMBERING NANETTE

Sadly, Nanette passed away on June 8, 2015, of colon cancer. It was discovered at a very late stage, and she wasn't able to go through chemotherapy. Losing her was the most heartbreaking loss I've experienced, other than the deaths of my parents. In her last few months she was at home in Tennessee, mostly confined to her bed. That's when it became even more clear how special she was.

Nanette and I had two visits together at her home during her final months, each visit for a couple of days at a time. Friends and family came to visit her as well and were welcome to stay overnight when they were from out of town. In fact, she had two calendars. One was to schedule local visitors, and the other was to schedule visitors who came from out of town, flying in from all over the country. Both calendars were full.

In spite of her illness, Nanette was still her upbeat, welcoming, genuinely caring self. She was honest about her illness and its likely outcome, which meant we didn't waste time tiptoeing around it. We were open and shared how much we loved each other and how much we appreciated our time together as friends and business partners. We talked about how my business had grown, primarily because of her, and what it had meant to our family. She cried and then said, "Of all the things I've done, I am most proud of my work with Coupon Mom."

We talked about her plans for her funeral. She loved her church with its weekly attendance of about a hundred people. Her family told her it would be too small to host the funeral, but Nanette wasn't concerned about that. She said they'd have to figure that out because she wanted her service to be in the church she loved so much. So it was.

On the morning of her funeral, we got to the chapel early to get a seat. Family and friends poured in, filling the chapel and the overflow area in the fellowship hall. There was one reserved pew that sat empty. Then a limousine arrived, and a line of New York television executives, including the president of a major network, came out of the car. They filed into the chapel and took their places in the reserved pew. They had flown in on a Saturday morning to the small town in Tennessee to honor Nanette, whom they loved dearly. Everyone loved Nanette.

Nanette went to college and majored in broadcast journalism. She was a stunningly beautiful blonde with big blue eyes and a brilliant smile. She could easily have been a television anchor; she could have been the star. Instead, Nanette made a life of supporting and loving people fully. She gave of herself to encourage others to take the stage, to help them be successful, to assure them that they were capable of anything, and that they were great at whatever they did.

She was an excellent television producer. After she left the *Today* show, she continued being a freelance producer for NBC and was called for many assignments over the years. She was known for being able to figure out the impossible. Her peers knew that if Nanette couldn't figure it out, they didn't need to waste their time trying to figure it out. Her friends told me those stories at Nanette's funeral because she would never have bragged about her abilities. There was even an A-list celebrity who required that Nanette be his producer, so NBC made sure that Nanette was assigned to his segments.

My one regret about Nanette is that we didn't spend more time together in person. We didn't live in the same city, and over all our years of work, we were probably together in person only six times. We could have gone on trips together, or I could have visited her just to enjoy being with her. We always talked about going on a spa vacation together or enjoying a weekend in Nashville. We always meant to do those things. But we were both busy with our careers and families. If I had made the time to see more of her in person, she would have too. We need to be intentional about spending time with the people we love, because we aren't guaranteed unlimited time together on this side of heaven.

Nanette taught me to be more generous in loving people. To be a better friend and to really care about what is going on in others' lives. Since her premature death at the age of fifty-five, spending more time with dear friends and relatives is a priority for me. Getting on airplanes to visit relatives and friends across the country is a privilege. Getting older isn't bothersome anymore, and having another birthday seems like a wonderful gift. Nanette's friendship was pivotal in my life—beyond her generous contribution to Coupon Mom. And I look forward to seeing her again someday, with plenty of time just to enjoy and love each other.

> **WE NEED TO BE INTENTIONAL ABOUT SPENDING TIME WITH THE PEOPLE WE LOVE.**

WHAT I LEARNED

Share the success. If you're lucky enough to have a partner like Nanette help you accomplish your bold vision, share the credit. You're a team, and you both contribute equally, though differently. Appreciate each other as copilots steering the plane together and respect each other's roles. Being a partner in a team and sharing the credit is much more rewarding than going it alone and taking all the credit.

Have real relationships. Love the people you work with and get to know them as the real people they are—in addition to interacting with them on a business level. When we love the people we work with, everything is better.

Take time to spend with the people you care about. You'll never remember the work you missed, but you'll never forget the time you spent with the people you love. Get on that plane, pick up the phone, walk next door. Ultimately, people are what matter the most to all of us. We never know how long we get to have each other here, so don't wait.

Unsung Heroes

THE COUPON MOM TEAM

The body is not made up of one part but of many.

—1 CORINTHIANS 12:14

In business expert Tim Schurrer's book *The Secret Society of Success*, he discusses the critical role people working behind the scenes play in every successful business. He describes the story of the person who operated the spotlight at a big country music star's concert. At one point the singer moved to another place on the stage that must not have been in the plans, because the spotlight operator couldn't follow him. For a few seconds, the singer was in the dark and the spotlight operator's role was very apparent to the audience. But until that happened, none of us would have given any thought to him, even though he was a critical person in the success of the singer's show.[1]

When those who work behind the scenes in your project

or business are doing their jobs, everything runs smoothly, and you may not even notice them. Because of this, it's even more important for us to recognize their contribution, because our work and our dreams will fall apart without them. Our people need to know how much we appreciate them. They need to know they are a critical part of the overall success. Even if you're the one in the spotlight, you need to remember it took a team to get you there.

> **OUR PEOPLE NEED TO KNOW HOW MUCH WE APPRECIATE THEM.**

FINDING THE RIGHT PEOPLE

In the twenty years of the Coupon Mom experience, we've had various levels of staffing, depending on whether we could afford to hire help. In the first three years the website did not have much traffic, and since its revenue depends on advertising, it didn't make much money. It earned enough to pay the minimal operating expenses but not enough to hire someone to do data entry. But the only way the site could attract more visitors was by providing consistent information. So even if we didn't have many visitors, we needed to provide great deals so I could promote the site's fabulous value when I spoke in the community or in the local media.

With so much experience, I knew what it took to keep the website's information going. It would have been much easier if grocery stores changed their prices only once a month! But the sales changed every week, fifty-two weeks a year. Looking back at that three-year period, I'm thankful I had to do the work myself. It taught me what my future team would be experiencing, so it's always been easy to appreciate all they've done for the past seventeen years. I have incredible gratitude for those who've faithfully kept Coupon Mom updated.

After my first *Good Morning America* appearance in 2004, the surge in website traffic resulted in our first $10,000 of extra revenue. But just having money to hire people doesn't mean it's easy to find the *right* people. Back then I knew very few people who even used coupons. The type of person who could figure out the best deals every week had to be more than a casual user. They needed to be varsity-level shoppers. They had to understand all the savings strategies and coupon caveats. They needed to think it was fun and exciting to put it all together—like a challenging puzzle.

I didn't know anyone who fit that description. I didn't know anyone like me. But I told one woman I knew who used coupons, and to my surprise, she told me about a club she belonged to in our area. It was called the Frugal Moms Club, and she offered to send the members an email describing our work-from-home data entry job.

As it turned out, the members of the Frugal Moms Club were the site's most loyal users. They had discovered it at the very beginning and loved it. They understood all the coupon strategies and thought it was fun. They were just like me! As the site grew, most of our staff members came from this club. They were easy to train, and they actually taught me more coupon tricks to share with our users. Even though each of the women had children, their work for Coupon Mom was consistent and always on time. Some of them got up before dawn to complete their work, and others stayed up past bedtime. They never missed deadlines, and they never complained. These women liked the work because it offered flexibility at a time when there were few remote job opportunities. This meant they could stay home with their young children and earn extra money for their families. All these years later, they use the extra money to pay for those children's college tuitions! I am extremely thankful for them.

People have shared life-changing experiences of saving money and avoiding financial difficulties because our service cut their grocery spending so dramatically. They've shared stories of donating food and supplies to charities in their communities and organizing large-scale efforts to teach the Coupon Mom strategy to others. The messages we've received have been emotionally overwhelming and filled us with gratitude.

Millions of shoppers have used the Coupon Mom website, and we've received thousands of emails thanking me for the service. (Since I was the only one visitors usually saw, they must have assumed I did all the work!) The site users were always thanking *me* because they didn't know all I did was talk about it in the media. The real heroes are the Coupon Mom team members faithfully doing tedious, mind-numbing data entry every single week. They've sacrificed time with their families and friends, and they've certainly sacrificed sleep. I would forward these stories to them so they could share in the joy. I hope they know what a difference their work is making in people's lives. Let me tell you about them.

THE COUPON MOM TEAM

Thank you, Mary Pat. She was the first one to work alongside me. She took on the most difficult store lists and entered the grocery coupons for thirty-one different cities every week. Mary Pat is calm, kind, and has never uttered one word of complaint. Did I mention she has three children, and one was a newborn baby when she started? She lived in our community for our first nine years together, and about eight years ago her husband took a transfer to a new city hundreds of miles away.

When she told me she was moving, my first reaction was complete panic. What would we do without her? And then she asked if it would be possible for her to continue working from her new city. Thank goodness—my heart started beating again. Yes, of course! Crisis averted. And then, if you can believe this, a few days later her husband came to my house. He said, "I just wanted to thank you for allowing Mary Pat to continue her work in our new city. We are so thankful for this job." Her work has helped millions of people—and I am so fortunate to have connected with her seventeen years ago. Words really can't describe how thankful I am for Mary Pat.

Thank you, Lisa. She came to our team via a friend of hers who worked for us first. Although her friend left the team after a short time, we are thankful that Lisa has stayed for fifteen years. Because she lives over a thousand miles away, we have only met in person twice. She was a quick learner and immediately went to work, doing a meticulous job. Lisa has an eye for detail and is a perfectionist. That's an important quality in our business, because if our grocery deals are wrong, it means thousands of shoppers will waste their time driving to a store to find a nonexistent deal.

Perfection is really important, so Lisa not only enters grocery deals but also checks everyone else's work to make sure we're accurate. Like Mary Pat, Lisa is also calm, kind, and never complains. Every time I thank her for her dedication, she turns it around and tells me how much she loves her job. We couldn't function without her, and I'm thankful she came to us from a thousand miles away—although I wish she lived down the street so I could see her more often!

Thank you, Amanda. Fourteen years ago Amanda's pastor invited me to speak at her church's Wednesday night meeting and dinner. I shared our Coupon Mom story with the group at the meeting, and then Amanda invited me to sit with her family for the dinner. I still remember how welcome they made me feel. We needed more workers on our Coupon Mom team, and Amanda was a savvy coupon shopper. I can't remember if I asked her or if she asked me—but she started working for us and enthusiastically took on our most popular grocery stores.

Amanda always stays current on the newest savings strategies and lets me know when it's time to add an improvement to the site for the benefit of our users. She genuinely cares about the quality of her work, and it shows. Her Publix deals list is a gold mine of savings for anyone who uses it. She spends more time on creating the list than she needs to because she wants to provide the very best service to other shoppers. You can't teach someone to care so much. It's just who Amanda is. Because she lives in our community, I've had the privilege of becoming friends with her. We have lunch together and share the details of our lives and pray for each other's situations. Sometimes we forget to talk about the website altogether! But when I have an idea for improving or changing the site, I always ask Amanda. I'm thankful she's been willing to be an unsung hero for all these years, as well as a dear friend.

Thank you, Robert. A brilliant software engineer, Robert heard through the grapevine that my website was having serious technical difficulties in early 2008. Since this was the start of a recession year, we were doing several Coupon Mom savings segments on local and national news. When thousands of people came to the website at the same time after a news story, the server couldn't handle the traffic and crashed. That meant that visitors got a blank screen and gave up in frustration. It was highly unlikely they would come back later, so our publicity efforts were wasted.

Robert had heard about this, and he sent me a simple email that said, "Can I help you?" He had a full-time job as a software developer. In his spare time on nights and weekends, he rewrote our software, fixed all the glitches, and improved it to the point that it never crashed, even on our highest-traffic days. I've never met anyone who works as hard as Robert, and I will be forever grateful to him for saving the website.

Over these past seventeen years there have been many more who have come along for this crazy ride. Kelvin Ling picked up where Robert left off ten years ago and has kept the website running smoothly ever since, receiving no user complaints. Many worked seven years or longer before moving on with their careers and lives. I am very thankful to Deann, Aileen, Carma, Shayna, Toni, Cindy, Nicole, Amy, and many others. They helped change thousands of lives. They helped change a little bit of the world. And they showed me what selfless loyalty and dedication looks like—without needing to be in the spotlight. Thank you sincerely—you've made my dream a reality.

There were also many who joined the team and stayed for about five minutes. The easy data entry job they expected wasn't easy at all. It was tedious, complex, and confusing. Working at home didn't mean it was easy. Their expectation that a work-from-home job would be easier than a job in an office made the reality even more shocking, I'm sure. Data entry can be tedious, no matter where you are when you're doing it. Those are stories for another day—but each failed attempt to add a team member was always a reminder of how incredible the people on our team were.

DON'T LET THEM BE UNSUNG. SING THEIR PRAISES.

So I'll say it again—you may be the one in the spotlight, which will probably be a lot of fun. But don't let yourself forget that you wouldn't be the one out front if you didn't have loyal, dedicated, hardworking heroes behind you. Don't let them be unsung. Sing their praises. Let them know how much you appreciate them. Share the success stories with them. And be thankful. I know I am.

WHAT I LEARNED

If you're the leader, don't take your team members for granted. It's easy to forget how much work occurs on a daily basis, especially when you're extremely busy focusing on growing and leading your business. Remember to acknowledge your team's work, to ask for their input when appropriate, and to personally thank them. People need to know their work matters.

If you're on the support team, remember you are playing an important role in the overall mission. It's easy to get bogged down in day-to-day tasks and discouraged when you're not feeling appreciated. Try to stay aware of the overall vision of the business and how important your role is to its success. Connect with your peers and reach out to your leaders to make sure you are part of the community.

Share the success stories. This applies to both leadership and support staff. Success stories come from multiple sources to various staff members. By sharing customer testimonials with leaders, support staff can help keep leadership connected to actual customer experiences. By sharing stories of closed sales or new deals with support staff, leaders can help them realize how their work supports the growth of the overall business. By sharing successes together, staff members at all levels feel part of a common team with a common purpose.

IF YOU DON'T FEEL CAPABLE, JOIN THE CLUB

> My God will meet all your needs according
> to the riches of his glory in Christ Jesus.
>
> —PHILIPPIANS 4:19

F ear is the emotion most likely to get in the way of our success. We all have plenty of fears—both rational and irrational. The Bible mentions fear more than three hundred times, so it's been a common human issue since the beginning.

There are plenty of rational fears—like getting a serious illness or something bad happening to our children or relatives. We can do our best to live healthy lives and keep our kids safe, but we can't control everything. So we do our best not to worry and to be thankful for each day we have.

Irrational fears paralyze us and keep us from pursuing our bold vision. Some of us are afraid of doing certain things that seem too risky—like skydiving, scuba diving, and rock climbing. I've been ziplining a couple of times, but I've never said, "I feel like ziplining today." Ever since the movie *Jaws*, the idea of swimming in the ocean is out of the question for me. There's no need for you to convince me why those are irrational fears, because they haven't gotten in the way of any of my daily activities yet. I can live with them.

WHEN FEAR DERAILS OUR VISION

What fears keep us from doing what we need to and from living life fully? You can google the list of most common fears in America and learn that many people are afraid of insects, snakes, heights, drowning, and needles. If you suffer from any of these, good news! They probably aren't going to get in the way of you pursuing your bold vision.

But if we're honest, we all have a fear of failure. Especially the fear of failing in front of people. That's probably why the fear of public speaking is the number one fear on most lists. We can debate whether that's an irrational fear or a rational one, but defining it doesn't really matter. Most of us have some experience with public speaking, even if it was just that terrible speech class you had to take in school. Most of us have felt the physical effects of that fear of public speaking—you feel shaky, your voice wobbles, or you might even break out in a sweat. And being afraid of those things happening makes us more

WE ALL HAVE A FEAR OF FAILURE.

nervous. Can you relate? Have you ever passed up an opportunity to give a presentation or speak to a group of people because of that fear?

Sometimes we have to do things that scare us because we care so much about our bold vision. We have to push through. If we don't, our path to success will suffer. But if we step into that fear and force ourselves to *do the thing that scares us*, incredible growth can happen. We will probably do just fine, we will survive, and we'll see ourselves differently afterward. That's the beauty of fear. Stepping into it and overcoming it can be exhilarating.

God says over and over again in Scripture, *Do not be afraid. I am with you. Just trust Me. I will never let you down, I will always be with you.*[1] That's quite an insurance policy. We can understand the concept and say we believe it, but it's quite a different story for our hearts to truly embrace it. That's why reading something every day to remind us of these promises is helpful—the Scriptures or a favorite devotional book. It's a daily practice we need, like charging our phones.

Over time these words will pop into our heads when we need them the most: God is with us. He's got this. He gave us this opportunity for a reason because He knows how much we care (and He cares) about our bold visions. Do not be afraid. As you pursue your bold vision, opportunities will come up that could change everything for your cause, even though they may terrify you. Don't let fear get in your way. Step right over it and see what happens. Saying no is not an option.

The idea of being on live national television was frightening. When the *Good Morning America* producer first took my call, my hope was that she would have the show's financial expert mention our website in one of the show's money segments. When the producer asked me to come on instead, the idea was exciting but also a little scary. Okay, it was terrifying! But the opportunity to get our coupon message to millions of viewers in just a few minutes was too good to pass up. The exposure could skyrocket the website's growth overnight. During that time, the local TV producer made his memorable statement about what going on *Good Morning America* would mean for us—that going forward, the Coupon Mom experience would always be divided between "before *GMA*" and "after *GMA*." He knew that national exposure would change everything for our cause, and he was right. Even though the idea of speaking to an audience that size was overwhelming, who wouldn't seize the opportunity?

> **DO NOT BE AFRAID.**

The plan was to film a shopping trip at a New York grocery store as a fun savings competition. The next day we'd air the shopping video and then do a live interview with the show's anchor, who'd also been present at the store, and answer questions. The segment would last six minutes, three of those consisting of the grocery store competition. That left just three minutes of live studio time answering a few questions in front of six million viewers. Three minutes sounded pretty easy—except for the six million viewers part. And the live part.

What would the right outfit be? Would my kids be okay while I was gone? How do you do the live studio part without getting dizzy, stuttering, forgetting what to say, or passing out? As silly as those questions sound, those are the types of fears that can paralyze us. They stop us from starting conversations with people who could have been friends, they prevent us from trying a new activity that could lead to new relationships, and they get us to believe the lie that if we take a chance, we will fail. But making a mistake doesn't end our journey on God's exciting plan for our lives. Just proceed, even if your knees are shaking a little bit. God's holding the door open for you—all you have to do is walk through it.

When we're afraid of something we have to do, we can try getting underneath the fear. We can break down the reasons behind the fear and try to solve them. For example, my friend always wore cute outfits. So before *GMA* she was happy to go shopping with me and help me find the right outfit. My husband made sure he was home to take care of the kids.

That left just the potential stuttering and passing out part to worry about. My mother didn't buy into those fears. "You've never stuttered or passed out before. Why are you afraid of that?"

"What if I start now?" I replied.

My brother is a very pragmatic business executive. His advice: "You are going on their show to talk about coupons. They're not going to ask you about anything but coupons. What in the world could they ask you that you don't know? It's your topic. Relax."

That actually made sense. When you're nervous or afraid about approaching someone regarding your project or presenting your idea to a group, it's important to remember that

> **WHEN YOU'RE NERVOUS ABOUT APPROACHING SOMEONE REGARDING YOUR PROJECT, IT'S IMPORTANT TO REMEMBER THAT THIS IS *YOUR TOPIC*.**

this is *your topic*. You could talk about it in your sleep. You are the expert, and that's why you're passionate about it. It's easy for you. Cross that fear off the list.

When we're going into a scary situation, it can be helpful to ask a friend to come. My dear friend of twenty-five years, Meg, agreed to meet in New York to go to *Good Morning America* with me. That really helped reduce the fear factor. She would make the whole thing funny. (And she did!)

The first step was taping the shopping trip with the show's anchor. That part was a breeze because it's what I'd been doing every week for years. When a show does a taped piece, you don't have to be nervous because they edit out any stupid things you say. We had dramatic savings at the cash register as planned and beat the anchor in the savings competition, which was the producer's plan. So far, so good.

The next day Meg and I got to the studio at the 6 a.m. call time for the live segment rehearsal, feeling like we were on a big adventure. We passed famous people in the hall and watched famous people go in and out of the green room where we waited. Who knows why they call it the green room? It's not green. We had lots of laughs. Having Meg there made it fun, calmed my nerves, and made it a shared experience we will always remember. Next time you're terrified of doing something, grab a friend if you can. And try to be there for that friend when they are facing a challenge and go through it with them. Life is so much easier and more fun when you can go through scary things with a friend.

LIVE ON *GMA*

The anchor reviewed her questions with me before the live segment started. The plan was that she would ask me a question about how viewers could save money, how to use the coupon system, and how to donate food to charity. How hard could it be? The questions were the same ones I'd answered a million times before. What difference would it make if more people were listening than usual? What was there to be afraid of?

When we're watching a news segment on TV, we see a set and a couple people talking. But what the viewers can't see behind the camera are dozens of people, lots of big lights, and multiple cameras all in a cavernous space with high ceilings. It's noisy with so many people in one place. Then, when the segment is about to start, the director counts down loudly (imagine hearing this when you're nervous): "Okay, everyone, *ten, nine, eight, seven, six, five, four, three . . .*" Then the red light on the camera goes on so you know the segment is live.

And the room immediately falls silent. You can hear a pin

drop. The anchor looks into the camera, smiles, welcomes America to the show, and explains what the segment is about. Then she asks questions, and the only sound in that huge space is the speaker's voice. It's surreal and understandably terrifying.

But here's what happened. Once the anchor asked the first question and we started talking about my favorite subject, time flew by. It was a blur. Pretty soon the red light went off and it was over, and no one stuttered or passed out. The anchor looked over and said, "You're a natural." I was so overwhelmed with relief and happiness that I threw my arms around her in a hug. (You shouldn't touch famous people, but I couldn't help it.) Meg got a picture of me hugging the anchor and it's one of my favorites, because it reminds me of the pure joy and relief of that moment. It was like jumping off a cliff and having God catch me in His arms.

We might not say everything perfectly, and we may look a little nervous when we get these chances to speak in front of others and share our passions. But no one will remember those details. You *can* do things that scare you, especially if you give yourself permission not to be perfect. *Perfection is not a requirement for being successful.* Repeat that three times! Most likely it will go fine, and fine is good enough for any of us. (And if it doesn't, you can always try again.)

PERFECTION IS NOT A REQUIREMENT FOR BEING SUCCESSFUL.

That was our one shot at national TV, I thought. I'd had the opportunity to explain our cause and coupon system to millions of people. If those six minutes were paid advertising, like a commercial, we never could have afforded it. But it didn't cost us anything. We just hoped a few people were paying attention.

The local TV producer was right. Everything was easy after that *GMA* segment on April 29, 2004. The website ads made enough money that we didn't have to give our idea away; we could build a team ourselves to grow it. People always returned our phone calls, and many new doors opened easily. Jumping off that cliff was the best decision, even if it was scary. God had a new, achievable direction that I never could have imagined, but He knew all the time.

But let's be clear. Overcoming the fear of going on live national television didn't mean I was perfect at it. In fact, I made many (not an exaggeration) mistakes over those seventeen segments. When you make a mistake on someone else's TV show, they let you know. In the early segments I used far too many words to explain my idea, and we ended up running out of time without covering all the planned topics. Another time I checked my luggage instead of carrying it on, and it was lost. So I wore an outfit and shoes from the anchor's wardrobe, but it was an inconvenience for the production team. They were kind enough to give me second and third chances at appearing on *GMA*, because apparently you don't have to be perfect to go on TV.

In the end, after two years the producers decided not to renew my contract. The coupon topic had been thoroughly covered, so it was the end of a good run. And to be honest, I didn't have the broad expertise that being a regular contributor required. There just weren't that many more ways to spin the coupon topic. Other regular contributors were experts in major categories, like finance, careers, parenting, and medicine, to name a few. But you know what? Being a permanent TV professional wasn't my bold vision in the first place. The show's couponing segments accelerated our goal of spreading the word about grocery coupons, and that was the bold vision.

Rather than thinking of the contract ending as a personal failure, I saw it as the end of a successful chapter. In fact, if it hadn't ended, the wonderful opportunities that followed would never have happened. The "failure" of not being renewed by *GMA* was actually a necessary stepping stone in the wonderful Coupon Mom journey. So next time you experience what feels like a setback, keep in mind that it may actually be leading you to the next giant leap forward on your journey. Our roadblocks are God's stepping stones.

I realize that now, but it took many years before hindsight helped me see that the producer's decision to end my contract was not because I was a failure. It's like trying out for the chorus in the school play and making it. You can either say "I made the chorus" or you can say "I failed. I didn't get the lead part." You were never going for the lead part! I didn't have the skill set to be a permanent part of the *GMA* team—it was a gift for a season. It was like being in the chorus for two years. Look at your experiences in the light of your original vision, and see them for the success they are. Don't move the goalposts and compare yourself to anyone else or you may be tempted to feel like you're a failure. And you're not. God has another step in mind.

We can choose to see ourselves through God's eyes, as His unique creation perfectly designed for the path He's showing us, or we can see ourselves as a failure simply because the path takes a new turn. Trust that there's a purpose and a plan for all the twists and turns. We aren't failing—we're following the One who knows where to go. Do not be afraid.

So how will you tackle the fears that impede your bold vision?

WHAT I LEARNED

Remember why you have the bold vision in the first place. You know it will help people. They need your help. By sharing your vision with others, you are giving them a gift. Step right over the fear so you can show up for the people who need to hear your message.

Remember that you are the expert on this topic—it's your vision. If you've put in the time and the passion, be confident in your knowledge, expertise, and conviction. And don't expect to be perfect. No one is perfect, and perfection isn't required to be successful.

Lean on the people who love you to support you. Talk to your encouragers, who probably have helpful things to say. My mother and brother encouraged me to go on *GMA* nineteen years ago, and their words have stayed with me. Ask a friend to come along if you're about to do something that intimidates you. Everything's better with a friend by your side.

Ask for Help and Share the Success

> "Ask and it will be given to you; seek and you will find; knock and the door will be opened to you."
>
> **—MATTHEW 7:7**

R obert, the developer who worked on the Coupon Mom site for years, had a history of successful entrepreneurial ventures beginning in middle school. He was hardwired to come up with creative, new ideas. His wife was a solo professional photographer, and he noticed that there wasn't a good online resource where photographers could upload and store their photos. Websites like Shutterfly serviced individual consumers with free storage, and there were expensive websites geared to prolific professional photographers. But there was no middle-market website offering affordable storage to photographers like his wife.

So Robert developed a website that met a practical need he observed for this middle market of photographers. He didn't think of it in a vacuum; he developed an idea that solved a problem for a specific segment of people that he understood. Ultimately, his website became highly profitable, and he sold it to another company. Now Robert is undoubtedly coming up with his next idea, and I'm sure it will be a solution to a problem he's observed.

GROWING A NEW IDEA

When we read the stories of entrepreneurs who've built successful businesses, it's easy to be amazed at their ingenuity and work ethic. Not only did they invent products that people loved, but they figured out how to have those products manufactured, distributed, marketed, and even patented. In many cases the entrepreneurs had no experience in any of those areas, but they were driven by their conviction to learn whatever they needed to so their product could help people.

> **ROBERT DEVELOPED AN IDEA THAT SOLVED A PROBLEM FOR A SPECIFIC SEGMENT OF PEOPLE THAT HE UNDERSTOOD.**

Many of us like to read inspiring entrepreneur stories—especially when it feels like the underdog made it big by helping people with something brilliant. Jamie Kern Lima developed a line of cosmetics and worked one hundred hours a week for years to build a successful company, which started in her living room and eventually sold for $1.2 billion.[1] There are many entrepreneurs who invented products, flew around the world to find the right manufacturers, worked long hours, and outsmarted much larger companies in the process of pursuing their dreams and building successful companies.

So to put our Coupon Mom business idea in perspective, our website matched grocery prices with available coupons to create a list of the best grocery deals, updated every week. We literally typed publicly available grocery prices and coupon information into a database that matched them up. It's called *aggregating* information, and frankly, it's not that hard. Certainly not as hard as manufacturing and distributing an actual product. In fact, it only took one Saturday for me, a person with no technical experience, to publish the website using a user-friendly software program. That's what they call a *low barrier to entry*, which means that ultimately, many people would start similar sites once free blog software became available many years later.

In 2001 I had to spend one hundred dollars on the software package, which was enough of a barrier to discourage many coupon users from starting their own website. On top of that, the weekly price updates required hours of data entry, which was undesirable for most people. Finally, coupon users like to get deals, and they don't always want to share. In fact, in the early days of my website, many users let me know they didn't appreciate that I was publicizing the best grocery deals. With a new influx of coupon shoppers, the stores would run out of the deals and the users didn't want to compete with others.

I ignored their opinion. In 2001 the unpopularity of grocery coupons resulted in unlimited free groceries for shoppers. There were plenty of coupons people weren't using and plenty of great deals that they weren't finding on their own. I couldn't be quiet about that. Providing this great information to every shopper in the country via a free website seemed like a great idea, especially when it meant we could help stock the food pantries with quality food.

There wasn't a clear path to earning money with a free website since today's major advertisers like Google AdSense didn't even exist yet. That gave us a seven-year head start before user-friendly blog software became available to many other coupon mom entrepreneurs in 2008. Earning money wasn't critical for me because websites are very cheap to run, and it was an exciting hobby.

But eventually we did need to find a way to make money to grow our efforts. Because we weren't selling a product, my challenge was figuring out how to earn revenue to pay for data entry people, marketing, advertising, and other staffing. I reached out to three similar websites in California, Ohio, and Utah. I spoke with each website owner and pitched the idea of referring site users to each other, since we each had grocery deals information for just our own states.

The other sites charged subscription fees, which started at sixty dollars a month. Needless to say, none of them wanted to link up with a similar website that didn't charge a subscription fee. Each tried to persuade me to charge a fee, saying that it wasn't fair to them that we provided this information free to users. One even said, "But you deserve to make money!" The word *deserve* felt wrong. The image of the mother waiting in the food pantry flashed in my mind. She needed our free help more than our family needed to make money.

One of the owners had her attorney send us a cease-and-desist letter, stating that our unsolicited business suggestions were interfering with her ability to manage her business effectively and if she was contacted again, she would sue me in a court of law (this was the result of two phone calls). Talk about putting out a campfire with a fire hose! An attorney's fees to fight a lawsuit were out of the question, so there were no more calls to her. I saved that letter in a file for years just for amusement. That letter was successful in causing me to abandon the idea of partnering with competing websites, which turned out to be the best outcome in the end.

Sometimes we feel stuck. If we had a drone's view of our overall path, we'd see that whatever obstacles we're facing are really just steps on the path. They're no big deal. Reflecting on that point in time nearly twenty years later, that's clear. Any partnerships or influxes of cash wouldn't have been helpful at that time because my idea hadn't evolved well enough. So when we feel stuck, we need to remind ourselves that we're just learning more. God is teaching us every step of the way. And learning more is critical as we pursue our dreams and efforts to help others.

When you are at a standstill financially, don't give up. You can start looking for creative ways to get your project off the ground on a shoestring. Seek out people or

> **GOD IS TEACHING US EVERY STEP OF THE WAY.**

organizations with similar goals and more resources, or find those with the professional skills you need who want to make a difference toward your cause as well. Link arms with people who care as much as you do about helping others with your idea. You'll build relationships at the same time as building your dream.

In time, there would be new ways to fund our website's growth with Google AdSense that ended up being far better than charging site visitors a fee or spending our family's life savings. It was a good lesson in patience and perseverance that mattered more than growing quickly. The free-website model ended up being the most financially successful long-term for us, and it clearly was better for the people who needed the help.

ENTER GEORGIA TECH

In the beginning each of the other grocery-deal websites were more user-friendly because they had custom databases. Our site's technology was clunky. We just published a long list of items on a web page, and if a site user wanted to print the list, they'd have to print many pages. The website could attract more visitors if the list was easier to navigate and could customize the database for each user. However, custom database development was cost-prohibitive for me back then before we had any advertising revenue.

A quick online search found an article about a group of students at Georgia Tech, a prestigious university nearby, who had developed a database for a local business. I called the professor mentioned in the article to ask if there was interest in helping with our website. He explained that yes, every senior at Georgia Tech had to complete a senior project, but each student decided what project they wanted to take on. He would throw our project in the hat, and we could see what happened. Frankly, he wasn't very confident that a college student would find a grocery coupon website interesting, but he agreed to give it a try.

A month later a Georgia Tech student named Karl called. He was the leader of a student team that had selected our project. Not one but four students signed up to work on it— Karl, Rick, Max, and Daag. They said it was because they wanted to be part of something that put food on people's tables.

It was so exciting—and hard to believe they decided to take on my project. For our first meeting, we went to lunch to explain the Cut Out Hunger concept and its potential to help people save money and donate food to charity. I was in full-sell mode. They responded enthusiastically and seemed really interested in helping. We discussed my ideas for site improvements, which was pretty much what the other sub-scription websites had. That was the extent of my vision for technology improvements. They listened politely and said they'd be in touch.

A few weeks later they invited me to come to campus to discuss the project. They asked several questions about our process of entering the price and coupon information, and the time involved. They explained that if we had a back-end database system, we would save time by eliminating repeated data entry each week. This was far more than I had requested, and it sounded like something that could easily break. We couldn't afford a regular developer to handle maintenance issues like that.

Plus, it was these students' senior year. I didn't want them to make the project too complicated because they should be having fun in their last year of college. At that point, one of the students stood up and said emphatically, "You don't even know what you need! Believe me, you need this. It will make your life so much easier. If we presented your minimal request to our peers as our class project, we'd be laughed out of the room. And working on this *is* what we think is fun! Let us do what we want to do. If you don't like it, you don't have to use it." Don't underestimate the work ethic and motivation of a Georgia Tech student.

Of course I agreed. The students' generosity with their time and skills was hard to believe. A few months later they demonstrated the system to their class for their final presentation and asked me to come. It was so exciting to see their ideas come to life. It was brilliant and would cut our data entry time in half. At the end the teacher and students asked questions. Then I raised my hand and asked if I could say something. The students reluctantly agreed to let me speak. I stood up and looked at the other students, who looked bored, and said, "This is absolutely amazing! This will revolutionize the coupon industry. No one else is doing this. It will change everything."

And it did. That database system is still in use on our website, twenty years later. It has been updated and modified, but the basic concept is the same. And yes, hundreds of websites copied its concept; even the coupon companies used it. The students' creative solution made using grocery coupons easier for the entire country. It was far better than the databases on the other websites, and it was entirely free to us. It was an incredible gift.

The students' approach teaches us not to be limited by what we see others doing. Rather than looking at the other websites as examples of the best technology, they (1) gave thought about what would help the situation, (2) identified the major limitations of the current system—repetitive data entry that could be reduced with a more sophisticated database, and (3) recognized the need for site users to have an easier shopping system. They didn't compare their product with anyone else's. They started at the beginning, asking, "How can we really help? How can we really make a difference here?"

As we pursue our dreams, are we looking to the right and left too much? Are we comparing ourselves to others doing something similar? Are we trying to be someone else? What if we started at the beginning and asked the most important questions: "How can we really help? How can we really make a difference here?" We can do that by taking into account what our God-given skills and talents are, not necessarily what someone else does well. That's the whole idea. Let's use what we were given to make a difference, because that's the only way we'll ever know how God wants to use us. That's the only way we'll ever experience His peace.

> **LET'S USE WHAT WE WERE GIVEN TO MAKE A DIFFERENCE.**

Once the website made money, we established a Cut Out Hunger scholarship endowment at Georgia Tech in the four students' names, allowing one computer science student to receive a small scholarship. Each year we get a letter from that year's scholarship recipient, and it warms my heart every time. The four students knew how important their contribution was, and they have each told me that they considered it the most important project they'd completed in their time at Georgia Tech.

If you are trying to start a project or business on a shoestring, you may find that a local university has student groups who are willing to contribute their time and talent to a cause they care about. You may find interested students across various disciplines, including finance, marketing, design, or computer science.

If you need staffing, you may find student interns who are willing to work for free in exchange for college credit. This can be an excellent resource to help you get started, and it can really make a difference in a student's career to get real-world work experience. Young people can bring the best ideas.

If you decide to go this route, remember that recognizing their contribution is important. It doesn't have to be an endowment if that isn't financially possible. Just show your appreciation and let them know they were contributors to your success, help them get future jobs with strong references, and let their professors know that they did a great job. And don't forget to thank God for leading you to the people who linked arms with you to help reach your dream.

THE COUPON COMPANIES

In the first year of the Cut Out Hunger website, I approached two coupon companies to try to convince them to take over my concept since I didn't have the resources to launch it quickly. They were intrigued with the idea, but both of the companies' executives explained it didn't fit with their business plan. On a personal level, they each thought the idea was good for shoppers and food pantries and asked, "How can we help you?"

Keep in mind that even in business, people are motivated by helping others. The executives saw the potential to use their influence to help feed the hungry, and perhaps to help this passionate young mother who felt compelled to share her idea with the world. They were kind, caring people who made a significant contribution in moving our cause forward.

This help came in two major ways: (1) They shipped weekly coupon circulars to my home in advance, which made data entry much easier, and (2) one of the companies offered us free advertising space. They created a nice full-page ad for our website, and every time a city's coupon circular had an empty space that hadn't sold, they used the Coupon Mom ad to fill it at the last minute. As a result, every single week for a few years our advertising reached millions of people across the country. If that space had been sold to advertisers, the total ad volume would have been worth millions of dollars.

If you believe in your cause and you can identify individuals or companies who have resources to help you, *don't be afraid to ask*. When someone can help you in a way that is easy for them, they get to experience the joy of giving and be partners in your success. Asking for help is ultimately a generous thing to do. Others get to be a part of God's journey and enjoy the satisfaction and peace of knowing that their efforts, even within the context of their paid profession, are helping people in a real way.

ASKING FOR HELP IS ULTIMATELY A GENEROUS THING TO DO.

On top of the coupon companies, one grocery chain was impressed by our website's mission and helped me in many ways. They funded marketing materials for Coupon Mom in several of our city's stores and took out a full-page ad about the website in the city's Sunday newspaper. They hired me to teach workshops in their stores, which helped pay for basic website expenses. They partnered with me and local food banks to publicize coupon food drives.

At the time, our business plan lacked the logical element of funding. But God's economy isn't always logical. When we were at a standstill, doors we never even noticed opened up. If I told a logical businessperson that major companies gave us millions of dollars of free advertising or that a university provided thousands of dollars of free software development—for a website operated from a spare bedroom—they probably wouldn't believe it.

When we look back at our experiences, it's easy to see that trusting God to open doors makes sense. As we go forward, we need to remember that He knows the best time to open doors for us. We may need to wait, but that's okay. The longer we wait, the more thankful we are to God when doors we never even expected open up to us. There are no coincidences. He's there with us the whole time. The more we see God working alongside us to help us, the more our trust grows and the closer we get to God.

WHAT I LEARNED

Ask for help, and trust the new ideas that others bring. If the Georgia Tech students had simply done the basic tasks I had requested, we wouldn't have been able to grow as quickly. They offered to help make a difference with their brilliance and hard work, which was far better than my limited ideas. When you ask for help, trust that the person you ask may have better ideas and then be open to trying their ideas.

When you ask for help, consider the potential benefits to the person or group you are asking. Although the coupon companies and the grocery company were generous with their resources, their businesses would ultimately benefit from our site's efforts to increase coupon use and shopping. Don't be afraid to ask for help if you believe there is a mutual benefit. Be prepared to explain and prove the mutual benefits to the people you meet with.

Share and celebrate your success with the people who helped you. Although the university and the companies provided the basis of the help we received, it is always people who personally help. People have feelings. Be sure to recognize, celebrate, and thank the ones who contributed to your success. The relationships you develop along your path are what you will remember the most. Making friends is where you'll find joy.

12

Two Words

KINDNESS MATTERS

Love is patient, love is kind.

—1 CORINTHIANS 13:4

G oing on the *Oprah Winfrey Show* to demonstrate the magic of couponing was like a dream. When the taping concluded, I hurried to gather my things and quickly leave. I reasoned that when you're a not-famous person and a celebrity is kind enough to let you go on their show, you should leave quietly and let them get back to work. It may be a monumental day in your life, but it's just another workday for the celebrity.

Just before I walked out the door, Oprah's producer ran up and said, "Wait! If you have time, Oprah always likes to have a picture taken with her guests. Then we'll send it to you."

Who wouldn't have time? This was unbelievable. Oprah

and I stood together in front of the big *Oprah* backdrop with our arms around each other. The cameraman was taking a few moments to adjust his camera, so we just stood there and waited. Very surreal.

She put her hand around my waist and pulled me close, then squeezed my waist. Twice. I counted. Then she turned to me and said, "Nice abs."

If you're a man, stick with this story for a little longer. If you're a woman, there's no need to explain. As far as I was concerned, God could take me right then. It would never get any better than this.

Just two words. But they carried a lot of weight in my mind, because Oprah said them to me. In those simple two words, she acted like we were both regular women who cared about the same silly things, like the state of our abs. Maybe I'm reading too much into it, and it just popped into her head and she said it. But it's more likely that she knows the weight of her words, and she chooses to use them to be kind. To be kind to everyone, even the ordinary mom who came to talk about grocery coupons.

I'd had dozens of appearances on big TV shows by that time, and no other host ever had a professional photographer set up to take a picture with guests. I wouldn't expect a famous person to grab me by the waist and pull me in, like a mother would do. Allowing me to talk about my business on her show was more than enough. Oprah probably said about ten thousand additional words that day, but I'm writing about just two of them thirteen years later. That's the potential weight of our words.

THE POWER OF WORDS

As we set our sights on our big dreams and ambitions, it can be easy to focus so much on our goals that we forget to be patient and kind to the people we encounter. Not everyone will have the same sense of urgency we do about our dreams, and everyone has their own pressures and stresses. Remember that loving people is God's overarching plan for our life, so be mindful of sharing positive words and holding back negative words as we pursue our goals.

Can you remember especially powerful words said to you, even if it was many years ago? Kind words and critical words, particularly from people whose opinions carried a lot of weight? They could come from teachers, parents, coaches, clergy, or friends. Can you remember specific positive words that motivated you to take a life-changing path? How do you feel about the person who said those encouraging words to you?

> **LOVING PEOPLE IS GOD'S OVERARCHING PLAN FOR OUR LIFE.**

Most of us will never know the impact, both positive and negative, of the words we have said to others. But we can focus on being more intentional so our positive words outnumber our negative words going forward.

A few weeks ago our women's group discussed what it looks like to try to act like Jesus in our daily lives. We had watched a video by a pastor who talked about how we are changed when we choose to follow Jesus; when we decide to accept His forgiveness, grace, and love. Knowing we are dearly loved and forgiven by this big God actually transforms us. As a result of believing that is true, how did we live differently, if we did at all?[1]

Each woman shared specific examples of how they acted and treated others differently because of their faith. Everyone said the same thing in different ways—that knowing we are loved by God makes us want to be kinder and more patient with others, who are also loved by God. Kindness doesn't always come naturally, but when we are intentional and practice being kind instead of allowing our initial reactions or responses to take over, we get better at it. And the best part is that in the process of trying to be kinder to others, in trying to make others feel better, we actually feel better ourselves.

One woman said that she approaches each day with an attitude of looking for opportunities to say kind things to people—to everyone she encounters. She looks for sincere ways to be kind because she doesn't want to be phony. As a result, she's much more aware and present as she pays attention to who she's around. She loves the people's expressions when they hear her words—their faces are instantly lit up by a smile. The best part of approaching her days this way is that, ultimately, it makes her happier. That's how love works. It's one of the few commodities that increases the more you give it away.

Jesus' brother James wrote about the power of the tongue (James 3). He talked about the power that such a small body part has to say both wonderful things and also evil things. He compared its power to a small spark that can set an entire forest on fire (v. 5). Left unchecked, the tongue, or the words we say, can corrupt a person's entire life.

Our son, Chris, worked at a large hotel at the front desk and encountered all kinds of people who said all kinds of words. We are reminded of the significant impact of words as he tells us entertaining stories from his workdays.

Once a man approached the desk and asked Chris for directions to the nearby conference center. He was a pastor attending a large conference for his religious denomination's annual meeting. This man was the president of the conference and was probably stressed because he was lost and could have been late. Chris tried to be helpful, but unfortunately the man said some hurtful words to him. Because he'd told Chris that he was a pastor and conference president, his words carried more weight than other guests'.

We can be sure that the man went on to give a meaningful and inspiring presentation at the conference, and he probably doesn't even remember his interaction with Chris. He was rushing and just wanted quick directions—he probably didn't see Chris as a twenty-five-year-old young man wondering whether the faith he'd grown up with was actually real. He didn't realize the power of his testimony that day. We understand because we are all human and don't always get it right.

We have all said a million words we wished we could take back. But that's not possible, so we need to ask for and accept that we're forgiven and move on. Instead of having regrets, let's focus on the opportunity to be transformed.

Let's be more intentional about using our words to love, everywhere, all the time. Let's try to be more conscious of carelessly using impatient, unkind words, even if we're only interacting with someone for a couple minutes and will never see them again.

"SHOW KINDNESS WHENEVER POSSIBLE"

One of the most important jobs for a front-desk attendant at a hotel is to make disgruntled guests happy. They call it *service recovery*, and it's the hotel's number one priority— particularly in this day of online service reviews. Talk about the power of words—online reviews have opened up a new channel of impactful words that will last forever. Chris is actually pretty good at service recovery and thinks it is a fun challenge. He said the easiest group of people to make happy, even if they are initially disgruntled, are women my age. His theory is that they probably have twenty-five-year-old adult children, so they are kinder to him.

As parents, we would all like to hug women like them and thank them for being kind to our children. Any parent knows how it feels when other adults are kind to our children, no matter how old those children are. If that's how we feel about our kids, imagine how God feels about all of us! How does it make God feel when someone is kind to one of His dearly loved children? How does it make Him feel when someone throws around hurtful words and bruises one of His dearly loved children? God loves us a million times more than we are capable of loving as humans, so we can only imagine that His joy or grief is that many more times what we feel.

My friend's approach of being kind with everyone she encounters is inspiring. We can all look for opportunities to say sincere, kind words to everyone we encounter throughout the day. It's fun—and makes us pay more attention. It lifts our spirits when we see faces light up as our kind words land gently. Simple words given generously prompt conversations that brighten our days and leave us feeling uplifted and connected. It's easy to give away kind words when we take this approach.

The greater challenge is holding our tongues from saying unkind words, and when we can do that, we feel even better than when we give away the kind words. A few weeks ago I had an experience that challenged me in this area. I was having a hard time finding a parking spot, and the only place available was a huge, overpriced lot. In desperation I paid the parking fee—in cash only—and parked. The attendant said to leave the keys in the car and leave it unlocked so they could move the car if necessary. They did not have numbered spaces and didn't give out parking tickets or receipts. The young man suggested taking a

> **WE CAN ALL LOOK FOR OPPORTUNITIES TO SAY SINCERE, KIND WORDS TO EVERYONE WE ENCOUNTER THROUGHOUT THE DAY.**

picture of the car's location to be able to find it at the end of the day. Talk about trust.

Returning at the end of the day, I looked for the car based on the picture, and apparently it had been moved somewhere else. No telling where. There were hundreds of cars packed tightly together, and I was driving a generic-looking rental car. I went to the attendant and, rather than saying what first came to mind (which is not printable), my new resolve surfaced. It stopped me and helped me hold my tongue.

Instead of unleashing those unkind words, I said, "Well, I like your system. Since I have no idea how to find my car, and all the cars are unlocked with keys inside, I'd like to take that nice BMW over there. They can find my rental car and have it."

The young man smiled. "That's not the best idea."

Surprisingly, we found my rental in less than a minute. It wasn't hard to find after all. Driving out of the parking lot, this overwhelming feeling of happiness came over me. My original, unsaid remarks probably wouldn't have meant much to the attendant because he was likely used to those comments. But saying those things out loud always makes us feel bad. Instead I felt happy—even slightly transformed.

The wonderful author Ann Patchett says it best: "Show kindness whenever possible. Show it to the people in front of you, the people coming up behind you, and the people with whom you are running neck and neck. It will vastly improve the quality of your own life, the lives of others, and the state of the world."[2]

How do you feel about the words you're saying every day?

WHAT I LEARNED

Look for ways to say kind words. Be intentional about saying a few sincere, kind words to everyone you encounter, even if it's just a moment in passing with someone you'll never see again. Say more affirmative words to the people you know well and speak to regularly. We're less likely to take our loved ones for granted when we make an effort to remind them of their good qualities or voice our appreciation for them.

Resist the urge to say unkind words. Resolve not to say hurtful words, even if you feel they are justified, and even if you won't see the person again. Imagine that the person you respect the most is watching what you say to people. And He is! God knows what we say to His children. Try to see people through God's view.

Pay attention to how you feel as you make changes. You'll probably feel better about yourself and realize you're loving people better. Let yourself feel good about being a kinder person and reinforce your own positive behavior.

13

Use God's Yardstick to Measure Success

We are not trying to please people
but God, who tests our hearts.

—1 THESSALONIANS 2:4

Tim Schurrer, the author of *The Secret Society of Success*, had a dream of becoming a famous country singer. He worked hard to get singing gigs and toured with another friend pursuing the same dream. As time went on, Tim realized he wasn't experiencing success as a singer, but he was honing his skills in managing the tour. Eventually he was hired as the operations executive for a business training organization. Today Tim is a successful executive running operations for an organization, and he has written a book about the value of being the behind-the-scenes support team rather than in the spotlight. He redefined his success measurement and experienced stellar success in a different role.[1]

DEFINING YOUR PERSONAL SUCCESS

What does success look like for you? When you imagine your dream coming true, what is the happy ending? How do you know if your idea is working? One of the advantages of coming up with a new idea is that there are no set expectations. You're not comparing yourself to someone else who has already done something similar, and you're not trying to keep up with anyone else's performance. You can make it up as you go.

But there's a reason you have this dream. There's something tugging at your heart, some change you want to make or someone you want to help. You have a hope, a goal, an endgame, and most likely it won't be perfectly measurable according to the world's standards. There won't be a report that measures the peace or comfort your idea may bring someone—including the peace and sense of satisfaction it may bring to you.

When we truly understand and articulate our idea of success, whether it's economic or intangible, it will naturally result in a sense of satisfaction and peace. So start by being honest with yourself about what success means to you. In my years of running a website, I met many other website owners with various definitions of success. For example, it's reasonable to measure success by an increased number of website visitors, which leads to more revenue. If the focus is simply on revenue, it's easy to forget the experience of the site visitor.

Websites may use whatever means possible to get people to click on their link, including deceptive headlines called clickbait. A headline may say "Double your money with this guaranteed investment plan" and get many clicks, but the actual website probably doesn't deliver on that promise. Yes, that click earned money, but it led to a frustrated site user. Is that success?

When you take the time to state your vision of success, you will avoid falling into the trap of continually moving the bar. If you keep moving your goal, you'll never feel you succeeded. Years ago, a friend of mine was in a commission sales job. He said that whenever he hit the sales goal for the year, the company would increase the goal the following year, without increasing the pay. The company may have thought they were being motivating, but my friend was only discouraged by the strategy.

We may do this with ourselves in setting goals for exercise, weight loss, or any other discipline. We may think if we reach the goal, then the goal must have been too easy. Rather than celebrating and being satisfied with success, we're harder on ourselves and set even higher goals. That's a recipe for frustration that can lead to a feeling of failure. Giving in to a feeling of failure can impede God's incredible plan for your idea. Consider what your vision of success will be and establish milestones for yourself as you put your idea into action. Most important, recognize when you experience success milestones and celebrate them. Acknowledging success helps keep us motivated as we work to make our ideas a reality. Have fun and celebrate!

HAVE FUN AND CELEBRATE!

For example, if you're trying to teach people how to do something, an obvious measurement is the number of people who agree to be taught and put your idea into action. At the beginning of the Cut Out Hunger idea, women came to my home for coffee and bagels and learned how to follow my coupon system to buy food for our local charity at no cost. By teaching more people, our donations multiplied. We were successful whenever we added another shopper.

After a few months we had about twenty-five shoppers throughout our community, and we considered that a major success. Of course, it was. It was twenty-five times more than we started with, and any business would consider twenty-five–fold growth in three months a huge success. Every next step was a thrill as we grew to hundreds of website visitors a month. Eventually the Coupon Mom website would have millions of members. Thankfully, we didn't have a crystal ball and couldn't see what the future held or we wouldn't have been so thrilled when our initial group reached twenty-five shoppers. Compared to millions, twenty-five shoppers would have been viewed as a failure. Instead, every little step felt like a huge success.

On the other hand, if we had compared ourselves to other charities or businesses that had thousands of supporters, we would have felt like a failure. That's the danger of comparing ourselves to others. Have you ever felt like you were doing well until you saw someone doing something much bigger? If we allow ourselves to get discouraged because we aren't running the exact same race as others, we can quit too soon. Defining our efforts as a failure and quitting too soon can be tragic, particularly when God may have had a wonderful plan in mind if we'd held on longer. It would be like throwing away the winning lottery ticket because the line to redeem tickets was too long. Don't miss out on the joy and satisfaction of all the small steps along the way by comparing yourself to something or someone else.

Sandra Stanley's devotional called *Comparison Trap* coined the phrase, "Not my race, not my pace."[2] Write that on a note card and keep it nearby. God has a unique plan for each of us, and He's given us our own unique talents and abilities. Even the athletic world does a better job making sure we aren't comparing apples to oranges. A featherweight fighter wouldn't be expected to compete with a heavyweight fighter. Every time we compare ourselves to someone else, we're making up a competition that God never intended us to have. Comparison never goes well. It either makes us feel inferior, which isn't good, or it makes us feel superior, which is even worse. I'm very susceptible to comparison and need to continually remind myself of this, because it can be the single cause of our dreams failing. And we are the ones responsible for this failure because we impose it on ourselves. Remembering "not my race, not my pace" helps set us free from the crippling effects of comparison.

God's economy doesn't use the same measurements the world does. Our little minds like numbers to track figures like sales volume, the number of customers, or the number of website visitors. But when we become too focused on numbers, we forget that each number represents a person, which is an entire life. When our hope is to change lives with our idea, we can't begin to know how God is using it in someone's life. We may see a report that represents that person as one visit to a website, but if we had a window into their life, we would see much more. That one visit to a website could mean one person was able to feed their family well all week long on a very limited budget.

GOD'S ECONOMY DOESN'T USE THE SAME MEASUREMENTS THE WORLD DOES.

How do you put a value on that? What is the value of a family enjoying eating together, without the stress of running out of grocery money? One website visit could be a high school student leading her youth group in shopping for a church food drive. How do you put a value on young people experiencing the joy of giving in that way? Or it could be another person inviting friends from her neighborhood to sit around her kitchen table as she teaches them how to use the coupon system. How do we measure the sense of satisfaction she has in being able to teach her friends something helpful? We have no idea how God is using our ideas, so we can't give in to the world's simple judgment of success based on traffic or sales reports.

IMPACTING ONE PERSON

Years ago I spoke to a group who had started coupon blogs similar to Coupon Mom. It was ten years after we began, and by that time our website traffic was at its highest point with millions of users a month. The new bloggers saw me as a pioneer in the world of coupon blogs. Some in the group had recently started coupon blogs, so they had relatively low traffic. Unfortunately, these people did have something to compare their blogs to, and their expectations were very different than mine had been when I started. Having twenty-five blog users would not have been a success in any of their minds. In fact, they were looking for answers from me, for a formula to quick success. My heart ached for them because they were working so hard and were discouraged. But many of them didn't feel successful yet.

The organizer of the conference had asked me to speak about time management. After sensing the bloggers' need for encouragement, I talked about God's measurement of success instead. How He is taking our ideas into people's lives and impacting them in positive ways that we'll never know on this side of heaven. We are taught to read and analyze reports, how to use data to shape our business strategies. We all agree business reports make sense, but we can't rely on them to measure our success in making a difference in the world.

The story of the woman who came up to me in the grocery store years ago proved that point. She introduced herself, held my hands, and said, "We are about to have a Hallmark moment. I discovered your website when my husband had lost his job and money was very tight. I learned how to feed our family well on a very small budget, and that helped keep us afloat for six months of unemployment. Thank you so much." All these years later, her sweet expression of gratitude still warms my heart.

Here's the thing. Her life experience couldn't be measured

by her one website visit on a report. Some of the new bloggers may have had only a few hundred visits a week, but God
doesn't see those numbers as merely website visits. Those
were the lives of real people, and regardless of whether
we are helping one person or one million people, the only
part that matters is that we are helping someone other than
ourselves. The measurement of our success isn't how many
people we reach but how well we can help others. And when
we help them, the life most changed will be our own. That's
success: loving others by doing what we do best, regardless
of how many choose to receive what we're offering. Success
is continuing to offer what we have, without counting how
many people show up. It's not about what others can give
us; it's about what we can give them. That's success, that's
love, and that's when we know we are making a difference
that matters. That's when we know we are following God's
path for our lives.

Scripture reminds us that no matter what we do, we should
work at it with all our heart as if working for God, not for
people (Colossians 3:23–24). Keeping our eyes on God's purpose for our journey will help us avoid distracting pressures.
When you look up to God, can you feel His approval? He's not the critic that people can be, because after all, He knows our potential and created us. He's your biggest fan, so stick with His perspective on your work.

HE'S YOUR BIGGEST FAN, SO STICK WITH HIS PERSPECTIVE ON YOUR WORK.

After that conference session, we all went out to dinner and stayed up late talking together in the hotel lobby afterward. We felt such a sense of community and love. We all cared about helping strangers with this crazy thing we loved to do, and we were all the same. Instead of being divided by how many visitors used our respective blogs—which is how the world would classify us—we were united by our genuine love for others and helping them learn what we loved to do. We had found our tribe—and we were all successful.

God's economy looks differently at how we interact. The world may label us as competitors—particularly in a business arena or any environment that pits us against each other in the effort to gain supporters or financial donors. Even the nonprofit world, with its noble humanitarian causes, can fall victim to this mindset as they feel they are competing for a limited pool of charitable donors.

What God really wants is for us to have community. Despite what the world may say, we probably have the most in common with our competitors. They are trying to do the same thing, and we probably share the same hopes and dreams. We're like little kids fighting in the sandbox over the same toy when we're surrounded by plenty of other toys. We could be enjoying so much more by playing together and taking advantage of more opportunities.

When our blogger group got together in the hotel lobby, I taught them things I'd learned, and they taught me many things I hadn't learned yet. We filled in each other's gaps. We shared our toys and had so much more fun doing that. We all experienced improved business results because we shared what we had. There were other bloggers who chose not to come to the conference because they felt we were competitors more than members of the same club. They missed the common bond and the shared community we all enjoyed that night. Don't miss that.

Competition and friendship are two sides of the same coin. Flip the coin and make a friend.

WHAT I LEARNED

Define your vision of success. If you are clear with yourself about what matters most, you won't get distracted by others' definitions of success. Your success measurement may be different than that of others in your field, but that's okay. It's your dream.

Measure your success. Even if your vision isn't measurable with business reports, you'll have experiences that let you know you're on the right track. Save the emails from people who let you know you're making a difference in their lives, and write down the affirming conversations to remind yourself that you're making progress.

Play to an audience of One. Remember why you have this vision. If you feel that it's inspired by what God wants you to do, look to Him for the affirmation and encouragement you'll need as you move forward. Resist the temptation to respond to people's benchmarks, which can make you feel like a ball in a pinball machine. Look to God and feel His approval for your sincere desire to make a difference. You'll feel more peace and less stress as you work toward your vision.

14

You Can't Take the Elevator to Success; You Have to Take the Stairs

Whatever you do, work at it with all your
heart, as working for the Lord, not for human
masters, since you know that you will receive
an inheritance from the Lord as a reward.
It is the Lord Christ you are serving.

–COLOSSIANS 3:23-24

In 2005 Dean Crowe of Marietta, Georgia, was heartbroken that her friend's son was fighting cancer. Dean asked her friend, "What can I do to help? And I won't bring dinner. This situation is way past dinner."

Her friend simply told her, "Raise money for childhood cancer research and fund the best research, wherever it may be."

With no experience in fundraising, Dean started taking small steps. Her group of friends presented their first $5,000 check to the boy's mother eighteen years ago. Dean formed the Rally Foundation as a 501(c)(3) to raise funding. Nearly two decades later, the Rally Foundation has awarded $25.4 million in research grants around the world.[1] One step, one stair at a time. Isn't that amazing?

It's only natural to want our big dreams to immediately get up and running. We visualize all the wonderful things that could happen if our ideas came to fruition, and we get excited about putting in the effort to make them a reality. As soon as possible. We may even fantasize about some influential person discovering our ideas and giving them an endorsement that makes them household names overnight.

When we have a dream, we can't help imagining that a big investor on *Shark Tank* or a celebrity would discover our product, service, or social cause and let the world know about it. A celebrity endorsement would make everything a lot easier. We could save so much time and work. That would be the elevator to success. Even though we all think we'd like the elevator better than the stairs, we may be wrong about that.

THE PATHWAYS TO SUCCESS

Here's my point. In reality, you probably won't be taking the elevator to success. You'll have to take the stairs. When you reach the floor you were aiming for, you'll have an appreciation for the level you reached because stairs take effort. Your success will be sweeter because you feel the work you put into getting there. You'll be stronger, because taking the stairs is much more exercise than pushing a button. You'll be more compassionate with the others taking the steps and build camaraderie with them as you make the long trek up. The most satisfying part of getting to the level you dreamed of isn't necessarily being there. It's all that happens during the journey. It's about who gets there with you. Those are the relationships, the memories, the experiences that matter the most. If we took the elevator, we'd miss the incredible journey of getting to our dreams.

Over the years, our Coupon Mom system has been featured by many national news shows. Famous people interviewed me and eventually millions of people joined our website. Yes, those media appearances were very helpful in raising awareness of what we had to offer. But if we hadn't been doing the hard work of developing and maintaining a helpful service, the site visitors wouldn't have come back. We had been "taking the stairs" for years before the first big media appearance, so television viewers were not disappointed when they took the time to look up the website. We had worked out the kinks and learned what helped shoppers most. Coupon Mom's greatest growth came from user referrals, which can only happen if what you're offering is helpful. It took years for us to refine and improve our service to make it easier to use. We took the stairs.

> **IF WE TOOK THE ELEVATOR, WE'D MISS THE INCREDIBLE JOURNEY OF GETTING TO OUR DREAMS.**

An interviewer once asked me what my most meaningful purchase was. Even at the age of forty-five, the answer didn't take too much thought. It was the new ten-speed bike I bought with my own money at age twelve. The bike cost $107, and it took hours of babysitting to earn that much. Back then mothers paid seventy-five cents an hour for babysitting—so $107 seemed like a million dollars. The highlight of every Saturday morning was depositing the week's earnings in my bank account and seeing the total in the bank book increase. Finally my mother took me to the bike store with my $107. Unfortunately, the sales tax made it $115, so it took another week of work to get the bike. At the time I don't know why my mother didn't pitch in the eight bucks. But looking back I realize that she knew it would mean more if I did the whole thing myself.

And it did. That bike probably had more miles on it than my first car. Riding it was always fun, and my parents kept it in their garage for another twenty-five years for sentimental reasons. It represented being able to reach a goal with determination and work. It represented the journey of succeeding—not just the end result of having something. It gave me confidence that with a strong worth ethic, it's possible to reach a goal, even if it takes a long time. That's what the journey to success is all about—and why it's so important to take the stairs.

> **ACHIEVING SUCCESS IS JUST PART OF THE PICTURE. GETTING THERE IS HOW WE GROW.**

Achieving success is just part of the picture. Getting there is how we grow. If my parents had given me a brand-new ten-speed bike as a gift, it would have been thrilling at the time. But I'm thankful they didn't do that. I'm thankful for the stairs.

LETTING OTHERS TAKE THE STAIRS

As parents, it can be hard to watch our children have to take the stairs. In fact, many of us are fantastic elevator operators! We jump in to help whenever we can, and we are happy when they achieve their hopes and dreams, even if it takes a little (or a lot) of help on our part. We can't bear to see our children experience pain and sadness. If there's something we can do to help them avoid pain, it's hard to stand on the sidelines and watch it happen. But sometimes our jumping in can rob our kids of the better path God has in mind. Have you ever been an elevator operator for your children or others?

I've done lots of jumping in. And in retrospect, our sons might have had a better journey without my interference. Fortunately, there were times when our sons took matters into their own hands before my husband and I could step in and mess it up, and they ended up with wonderful outcomes we couldn't have predicted.

When our son David was in high school, he was cut from the baseball team. This was a big disappointment, and as soon as we heard, my husband, Dave, and I started thinking about how we could get this turned around. Our son got the news, and instead of feeling sorry for himself, he immediately picked up the phone and called the soccer coach to see if it was too late to join the team. The coach said he'd be happy to have David join.

As it turned out, David loved soccer. He played three years, and in his senior year the soccer team won the state championship. Ten years later, a friend of his from the soccer team had David as a groomsman in his wedding, and David had him in his wedding too. That soccer experience led to a lifelong friendship. His success looked different than he originally expected, but sometimes that's the way God works. He surprises us with new paths that are even better than our original plans. That doesn't mean the original plan was wrong. It just means there can be more than one route to success.

I once read this advice: "Do not get in the way of God's plan for someone else's life." That puts our well-intentioned interference in perspective. Who knows what we're robbing our children of when we jump in to control their circumstances? Who are we to play God in their lives?

When my cousin was a senior in high school, she saved her money to pay for her college application fees because she wanted to send in her applications without her parents knowing about them. She didn't want her parents revising her college essays. Her parents are extremely loving parents who are also good writers. She knew they'd want to make changes, and then she wouldn't feel like she was getting into college on her own merits. So she wrote essays, filled out the applications with no help, and must have included cash payments since none of us had checkbooks at that age. And yes, she got into all the schools, graduated with honors, and went on to earn her master's degree and PhD. My cousin is a brilliant college professor today. Although her parents would have helped her because they wanted the best for her, sometimes the best route is to let our children experience their own success, even if that means experiencing failures too.

Whether we succeed or fail isn't the end of the story. Specific successes and failures along our journey are simply steps toward our successful vision. They shape us, they build character, and they help us become the people that God sees us to be.

PERSISTENCE TOWARD GOALS

The truth is that if we want to reach our dream, if we want to experience our vision of success, it's going to take a lot of work. It will test us and show us whether or not we really care about that dream. If you believe that God has shown you your dream and is inspiring you to pursue it, don't go it alone. We need to tune in to God, spend time with Him in Scripture and prayer, and continue to look to Him and pray for His guidance and support. We need to lean on Him and pay attention to how He is leading us on our journey up the stairs. When we hit obstacles, we can turn to Him and be honest about our frustrations. When we have successes, we can thank Him and believe that He's celebrating with us. When people criticize us for our crazy dreams, we can remind ourselves that we are working for Him, not to please people. There may be many critics—there were for me—but when you know you are doing God's work, you won't get discouraged by them. If you know God is for you, that's enough to get you up those stairs.

IF YOU KNOW GOD IS FOR YOU, THAT'S ENOUGH TO GET YOU UP THOSE STAIRS.

It can be very helpful to have encouragers, team members, or partners to help you up those stairs. It can be really difficult to do it on your own. You do not necessarily need an official business partner with financial ties; people can come along beside you because they see your vision and want to join you. That gives us even more fulfillment when we can share our journeys with others who come alongside us.

The story of Jack Canfield, author of the *Chicken Soup for the Soul* books, is very inspiring. I heard him tell his story like this.[2] Years ago he was a high school teacher and had written a book for teachers on how to give students self-esteem, since they weren't likely to learn in school until they had confidence as students. He did quite a bit of motivational speaking at teacher conferences and told many stories to illustrate his points. After appearances, people would ask if they could buy his book of stories. Well, he didn't have a book of his stories, but that question prompted him to write one. He wrote about sixty stories and was ready to try to get it published. A colleague and friend, Mark Hansen, said, "No, you need 101 stories—that's a number that will sell. I'll write forty-one and join you." Jack initially thought he didn't need a partner, that he'd already done most of the work. But he agreed, and then they had a manuscript ready to be published called *Chicken Soup for the Soul: 101 Stories to Open the Heart and Rekindle the Spirit.*

Jack and Mark signed up with a literary agent, who sent the manuscript to twenty-two publishers. Unfortunately, every publisher rejected the manuscript. Many of them didn't like the title. The literary agent resigned. So Jack and Mark began going to publishing conferences and approached publishers personally. Together, they were rejected by a total of 144 publishers. Yes, you read that right. Would you be able to continue going to publishers after that many rejections? It seems that 10 or 20 rejections would be enough for most of us to find a new hobby. Maybe 50, maybe 60, but 144?

Perhaps because they had each other, they probably encouraged each other to keep trying. They were both motivational speakers, after all. They probably had all kinds of great stories about pursuing your dreams. Scripture tells us two are better than one, that when one falls, the other can lift them up. But woe to the person who doesn't have anyone to lift them up (Ecclesiastes 4:9–10).

Fortunately for millions of people in the world, they did have each other for encouragement. We can imagine that when one wanted to give up, the other talked him out of it, and vice versa. Finally, publisher number 145 said yes. Jack said it was a small health and wellness publisher in the Southeast that was struggling and was about to go out of business. That small publisher threw them the life preserver they needed, and their book was published in June 1993. It was a runaway bestseller by the end of the year. Their single book sold eleven million copies around the world. They went on to publish 250 different versions of *Chicken Soup for the Soul* books. As of this writing, their line of books has sold more than 500 million copies. Jack Canfield has had forty-seven *New York Times* bestsellers since then. There are *Chicken Soup for the Soul* podcasts, TV shows, YouTube channels, apps, and even a line of pet food.[3]

So don't quit at 144. Look at all Canfield and Hansen would have missed, at all the world would have missed, if they had given up on their dream. They had a dream that the world needed. God knew that. Two friends held each other up. A stranger threw them a life preserver and joined them on their journey. And we can imagine that Jack and Mark would say their journey up those stairs made the success far sweeter than it would have been if the first publisher had said yes. And publisher number 145 must have been very happy that Jack and Mark didn't give up at 144!

WHAT I LEARNED

Stay connected to God through your journey. Many of us feel inspired by God when we discover our dream, but it's easy to focus on the work of the journey and get too busy to spend time with God. He's our best encourager, and staying in touch with Him is like charging our phone every day. We need to recharge our soul with Him to get up those stairs.

Lean on trusted people for encouragement. There will be people in your life who catch your vision and will want to help you along, both actively and spiritually. When you get discouraged, reach out to them, and take their words of comfort and their offer to pray for you and your dream. Encouragers got me through very difficult times, and their support made the difference between quitting and getting to the top of the stairs.

View failures as part of the journey to success. There will be discouragement and seemingly clear messages that your dream isn't possible. With hindsight, it's easy to see failures as temporary setbacks on our journeys. However, when we're in the middle of those temporary setbacks, it's tempting to give up. When that happens, go back to God. Remember why you started this journey in the first place. Remember that publisher number 145 is just around the corner. There are people who need your dream to succeed. Don't miss it.

Just One Person

> "Let your light shine before others, that they may see
> your good deeds and glorify your Father in heaven."
>
> —MATTHEW 5:16

"A re you okay with this?" asked Pastor Mark Batterson.

Batterson, pastor of National Community Church in Washington, DC, spoke on how we can become "unstuck" in our lives by helping people suffering from poverty around the world. He shared compelling statistics: Twenty-five thousand people die per day from starvation and malnutrition around the world. One child dies every twenty-one seconds from drinking contaminated water. There are millions of children living without families—orphans—around the world. With each statistic, he asked the audience the question "Are you okay with this?"[1]

The truth is, we're not okay with that. But the magnitude of suffering seems overwhelming. We hear statistics like these, we see people in our own country suffering from the aftereffects of natural disasters, we see homeless people on the streets in our own cities. To be honest, many of us deal with these seemingly insurmountable problems by looking away. We can't solve them, so we don't want to look at them. We are just one person. What difference can we really make? So we look away and go on with our lives. Have you ever felt this sense of helplessness in the face of overwhelming suffering? Do you ever look away? I know I have.

CHANGED BY POVERTY

Blogger and mother of three Kristen Welch wrote a wonderful book called *Rhinestone Jesus*. I read it on a long airline flight, and by the time we landed, it felt like my life perspective had changed. There's no way you can finish that book without wanting to do at least one small thing to help. It's a story about how she went on a mission trip to Kenya with a group of mom bloggers. Compassion International is an organization that sponsors children and orphans all over the world, and the organization sponsored this trip so the bloggers would share their experiences with their readers. Hopefully, the bloggers' stories would inspire their readers to sponsor orphans.

In Kristen's book, she describes her unexpected experience of being so changed by the poverty she saw that she ultimately built a residential program for pregnant single mothers. Kristen was a stay-at-home mother of three in Texas with a comfortable life, but not excessive by US standards. When she came home, she was disturbed by the stark contrast between her comfortable life and the orphans' poverty. Rather than looking away, she decided to do something about what she saw. Today, more than ten years after that first visit to Kenya, she runs a successful organization with the sole mission of helping women in developing countries support their families with dignified jobs, food, shelter, and medical services.[2]

During that first visit to our community's food pantry twenty-one years ago to donate the free groceries purchased with coupons, I sat in the waiting room with clients of the food pantry for half an hour. Fortunately, waiting with them was the best thing that ever happened. That was the moment statistics became real people. Rather than just hearing a statistic like "one in five children goes hungry in our city," a mother like me with children like mine was there too. Perhaps her children would have been that statistic if there wasn't a food pantry for her to visit. *Poverty* went from being just a word to being a mother like her. The only difference between us was that we lived in different circumstances. We both loved our children but only one of us had to worry about whether her children would have dinner each night. That first experience led to our Cut Out Hunger initiative, to the Coupon Mom experience, and ultimately helped millions of people donate food to their local food pantries. It didn't happen overnight; it happened one step at a time. It started with just one person with a crazy idea. But it worked.

> **WHEN STATISTICS BECOME PERSONAL, ALL BETS ARE OFF.**

When statistics become personal, all bets are off. Any hesitation about being "just one person" who can't make a difference goes out the window. Our hearts get involved. We want to help. It's no longer a "I should help" kind of thing. It's impossible to look away, and we can't get to work fast enough. And the best part is that it doesn't even feel like work. It feels like purpose, and having an important purpose feels pretty great. We wonder why it took so long to find it. We wonder why we ever looked away.

Have you ever had a personal encounter with people suffering from poverty, natural disasters, or medical crises that changed your perspective? Did you take action? Did you feel a clear sense of purpose? If so, you understand what we're talking about.

Perhaps you haven't been directly involved in helping these types of causes yet. Finding something that really matters to you may be the first step on your new journey. Remember to ask yourself, as Pastor Andy Stanley asks, "What breaks your heart?" When we can answer that question, we know where to start. Getting involved in an area that appeals to your heart can be a great way to use your God-given talents and abilities. Not only can you make a difference in others' lives, but you'll also experience a sense of purpose and fulfillment that will change your life.

An understandable reason people don't get involved in trying to help others suffering from poverty, illness, or other social injustices is that it isn't realistic for most of us to build an orphanage or a school in a developing country. We need to support our families, pay the bills, and raise our children. Those responsibilities are almost more than we can handle now—it's hard enough to get the housework and grocery shopping done each week. Adding a major charitable initiative is just not possible. But that's okay. There are plenty of ways we can help people that will fit into our lives. We can start by asking ourselves a few questions.

The most important question isn't "what?" The most important question is "when?" Starting now is the important part. Just step into something that helps people, and you'll see what the next step is after that. One step at a time. You don't need a complicated plan. You just need to take a step. As Pastor Mark Batterson said in his talk, "You can't walk on water if you don't step out of the boat."[3]

After reading Kristen Welch's book and interviewing her on my podcast,[4] the next step was easy. She's such an inspiration in all she has done, and she wants to encourage others to take their next step toward helping others too. But she isn't trying to convince people to do what she has done. She's trying to encourage others to take a first step based on their capabilities right now. In her chapter "Start Small Today," she suggests a few easy steps. One was to sponsor a child through World Vision or Compassion International. That was something my husband and I could do, so that's where we're starting. It's easy, and the total cost of monthly sponsorship for one child is less than my cell phone bill for one phone. That's right. We can literally give a future to a child for less than forty dollars a

> YOU DON'T NEED A COMPLICATED PLAN. YOU JUST NEED TO TAKE A STEP.

month. Both organizations are highly rated by the watchdog organization Charity Navigator, so we can give with confidence that the children are benefiting from our donations. Even better, we can communicate with the children by sending them letters, which means so much to them—and to us. We can love them easily in a few ways, right from where we are. We don't have to go all the way to Kenya to show love to them. We only need to take one step.

ANYONE CAN INSPIRE CHANGE

Kristen Welch is one person. When she came back from Kenya, she reached out to the loyal followers of her blog. They gave money to help build the residential program for women in Kenya. Over the years, as financial needs arose, blog readers responded generously to help meet their needs. Kristen may have been one person, but because she shared her story, her inspiration, and her genuine love for the people they were helping, she naturally inspired others to help her too.

People with inspiring visions become leaders. They become more than one person—they become an army. You may have a similar story when you find a purpose that matters to you. The wonderful part of inspiring others to give is that you make them part of the story. They get to share in the joy of helping others in a way that makes sense in their lives. Kristen thinks of her family as a conduit of God's gifts, with both hands open. One hand receives gifts, and the other hand gives them to the women in need. God can use us as conduits. We don't have to be the source of all the money, energy, or other resources necessary for our cause. In this way, Kristen is ministering to two groups of people. She's enabling her blog visitors to experience the joy of giving, and the Kenyan women are experiencing thriving, healthy, productive lives. Kristen has the joyful, though exhausting, blessing of being a conduit to help meet God's purposes. Similarly, you may discover an opportunity to be a conduit for God's purposes in your world.

To be honest, when the idea of sponsoring an orphan first came to mind, my next thought was, *But there are millions of orphans. How much difference can sponsoring one orphan really make?* I'm not proud of that thought, but it's worth sharing because the next thoughts mattered more. When we picture millions of nameless orphans, it's like hearing statistics. But if we can imagine just one of these children, we can think more about why they are an orphan. They each have parents who are no longer living. Each child was someone's entire world.

What if we died and our child was one of those orphans? What if we were able to see our children from heaven, alone in the world? Wouldn't we be hoping and praying that a kind person would step in for us because we couldn't? And we have the opportunity to step in for those parents. We have the opportunity to answer that mother's prayer. So now I like to visualize her and how she would feel knowing her child was being sponsored. Who knows how heaven works exactly, but maybe one day we'll meet. That thought makes me happy and helps me realize that just one person is enough. I'm just one person, and that precious child is just one person. You are one person. We're all more than enough.

WHAT I LEARNED

Read other people's stories. We can learn so much from people who are like us and have experienced success in helping others, even though they did not have unlimited resources. Inspiration helps us find the dreams we are made for.

Start small. A small step for you may be a big step for the person you're helping. Start by helping one person. Do something that comes easily to you. Ask friends about causes they care about. There are so many needs that you can start trying to meet in just a few hours a week (or a few hours a month if that's your availability). Whether it's tutoring children, making sandwiches for the homeless, or volunteering at a food pantry—your time and effort will make a difference in someone's life that day.

Ask God. Pray for God to show you where you can make the most difference with your talents and abilities. Then pay attention—He'll show you. And it may be the best thing that's ever happened to you. Prepare to be surprised. All it takes is getting out of the boat.

16

Playing to an Audience of One

KNOW YOUR AUDIENCE

Brothers and sisters, we instructed you how to live
in order to please God, as in fact you are living.

—1 THESSALONIANS 4:1

After my mother passed away in 2010, my stepfather began reading her Bible every day. She had written notes in the margins of some Bible verses. One day he called to say she had written "Cut Out Hunger" next to Colossians 3:23. The verse said, "Whatever you do, work at it with all of your heart, as working for the Lord, not for human masters." If she had said that to me in person, it would have meant a lot. The fact that she had written it privately was even better. It was a sweet message from her that I will always cherish.

When the Cut Out Hunger idea first hit, it completely changed my life outlook. The new awareness of how many families in our area struggled with food insecurity woke me up and made me want to do something about it, as soon as possible. That energy, combined with the absolute conviction that this was what God wanted me to do, propelled me to pour all my spare time into working on it. Delivering groceries to the food pantry was exciting and emotional, and it energized me to teach how to shop for the food pantry too. It literally felt like God was with me—while driving our minivan stocked with food and listening to Christian music on the radio. It felt like working for God, and it filled me with joy.

FINE-TUNING OUR FOCUS

Whatever we do, we should work at it with all our heart because we are working for God. We are playing to an audience of One. When we focus on what He wants for us, how He wants us to help others, we know what to do. We know who we are, and we don't have to be concerned about people's expectations and opinions, which can be so distracting and confusing. If we know we are following God's lead, we can work for Him. Not only will we be helping others as He wants us to, but we will be filled with joy because we know He's pleased with us. We know He loves us, and He is pleased because we are showing His love to others.

When you are pursuing God's path and believe you are following His purpose for your life, look to Him as your guide. We have a clearer vision when we truly believe we are working for God rather than trying to impress or please others. When we focus on performing for people, insecurities naturally surface. When we focus on working for the God who created us, who knows us and loves us, we can relax into our purpose.

It's easy to get side-tracked when we feel like people are disappointed in us. We naturally try to make changes to make sure everyone is satisfied with whatever we're supposed to be doing. It doesn't always work, particularly when there are multiple people

> **WE HAVE A CLEARER VISION WHEN WE TRULY BELIEVE WE ARE WORKING FOR GOD.**

involved and they all have opinions. This can happen when you're leading a group of people—whether it's a work team, a committee, or even a volunteer project. One time a member of a group I was leading seemed to be disappointed in how the group was going. When we made a change to accommodate her suggestions, something else would come up that wasn't quite right. It felt like I was failing as a group leader. It was probably more about my sensitivity as a new leader than her comments, but it started to bother me and take up too much mental space outside our group meetings.

Then a friend named Amanda came on my podcast, *Pivotal People*, and shared how she is able to have hope, joy, and peace in the midst of a serious illness.[1] Her hope and joy are overflowing, and she is one of the most inspiring people you'll ever meet. She explained how she'd broken a hip and had to undergo physical therapy. As she was learning to walk again, she'd look down at her feet to make sure she didn't trip. The physical therapist told her no, she needed to look up and focus her eyes about ten feet in front of her. If she looked at her feet, she'd probably trip. By looking up and away from her feet, she'd see where she was going, and she wouldn't trip.

It sounds counterintuitive, but it actually worked. Amanda used this as a metaphor for how we are with God. When we look down at our feet, that's like looking at our day-to-day circumstances that are troubling us. We get caught up in them and they cause us to trip, to sink into despair. But if we look up to God and keep our eyes on His lead, we see hope. We can rise above our troubling circumstances when we keep our eyes on Him and His love for us.

> **WE CAN RISE ABOVE OUR TROUBLING CIRCUMSTANCES WHEN WE KEEP OUR EYES ON HIM AND HIS LOVE FOR US.**

That rang true for me. The group member's complaints were a minor issue, but when I was focusing on them and evaluating my performance by them, it was easy for me to feel bad. When I looked up to God for His assurance, it felt like He was okay with my efforts. It felt like He knew I was trying my best. Once that realization hit me, my stress about the group's dynamics evaporated. When we look up and realize we are working for God, not for people, it's like a weight is lifted off our shoulders. We can be compassionate about people's dissatisfaction, but we don't have to let it manage us. We can look to God for His direction and be at peace with our performance. We are playing to an audience of One.

'GETTING TO KNOW OUR AUDIENCE OF ONE

There may be times in our lives when having God as our audience may not sound appealing. Maybe we don't really want God watching. Perhaps we make choices that are attractive at the time, but God might not think they are the best for us. Or we don't want to give up any control over our decisions, or get wise input about them, because we really want to do what we want. We're like children who are willing to get grounded for the sake of having the fun of breaking the rules occasionally. Hiding from our parents here on earth can work, but it never works to try to hide from God. He can see everything. Just because we close our eyes to Him doesn't mean He ever closes His eyes to us. But He's patient. He probably knows we'll be coming back to Him for help getting us out of our mess later. So He waits.

Imagining God as our audience can also be hard if we don't know Him well enough. If God feels far away from us, it's hard to feel connected to Him as our guide. We all agree that we need to really know our audience to do our best work. Any salesperson or performer knows that the key to being effective is to know their audience. If selling widgets effectively depends on whether we know the audience, can you imagine what a difference it would make if we really understood what

God is like and who He is? If we knew and trusted Him, we could rely on His grace and acceptance instead of the erratic opinions of people giving us inaccurate performance reviews. God knows us better than anyone and believes in us more than anyone. Given the choice, most of us would rather have His assurance and approval than people's criticism.

GOD KNOWS US BETTER THAN ANYONE AND BELIEVES IN US MORE THAN ANYONE.

So how do we get to know Him? Where do we start? We can begin by understanding how we see God now. Who do we think of when we think of God? That's an important question to ask ourselves because our connection to God comes down to how each of us views God. Our perception of who God is and how He relates to us makes all the difference in whether we want to connect with Him at all. Pastor Jamey Dickens gave a sermon about the various ways people see God. His characterizations resonated with me, so I've added detailed descriptions here. You can watch Jamey's original sermon to get the full story—it would be well worth your time.[2] Do you see God in any of these descriptions?

- **God as a Referee.** The God who is watching our every move and calling fouls whenever we mess up. He is a constant judge, and He can put us on the bench if we don't perform well. He has our name on a list and He's keeping score over the course of our lives, keeping track of our good deeds and our mistakes. We'll find out at the end how we did. In the meantime, it's best to keep our head down and try not to call attention to ourselves.

- **The Alexa God:** He's there to answer our questions and requests. When we need Him, we can ask. He knows everything and He can do everything for us—if He wants to. Ask nicely.

- **The Old Man God:** He's nice and sweet, but He's not really up on the current issues of the day. He doesn't understand them, and He's not relatable. He's disconnected from reality, but He is a kind old man.

- **God in the Clouds:** He created our world and He's far away and mysterious. He's hard to know, although educated religious leaders like pastors, rabbis, and priests may know Him. He's too distant for regular people like us to understand.

- **The Fairy Tale God:** The stories we hear about God are nice, but they don't seem realistic. Maybe the whole thing is a made-up fairy tale. We don't need to decide whether it's true or not, which is good because we are busy with all life's daily issues and responsibilities. We'll leave that up to other people.

Pastor Dickens acknowledges that most of us have seen God in one or more of these ways at various times in our lives. And if this is how we see God, it stands to reason that we wouldn't be connected to God. Either we are afraid of Him, or we don't see how we could ever connect with Him. Why would we want to get to know the referee? We want to avoid Him. The Alexa God is fine when we need Him, but that's not a friendship. We can't relate to the other versions of God, so becoming friends with them doesn't make sense. We don't really think about God too much. We let others be our audience, and they are more than happy to run the show.

Dickens goes on to talk about how God is most like a loving Father. When we think of how earthly parents love their children, imagine how the God who created us feels about us. When we get to know God, we can experience a relationship with Him as a trusted Father who loves us unconditionally. When we get to know God, it changes our entire life.

Trying to get to know God personally became a priority when I quit my corporate job to stay home with my two young children. It was easy to join a mother's group at church and start a Bible study for the first time. When a teacher was explaining concepts and we were following a workbook, it made more sense than if I'd just opened the Bible to read it myself. Plus, it was a great way to meet other women in my same situation, and we became friends. Over the years, signing up for Bible studies became a fun and easy way to learn more about God and get to know people who were interested in talking about God. That's fellowship, which is a good way to get to know God too.

There are also many easy ways to learn more about God on your own, without having to attend a study. These days, hundreds of online video series are available, produced by excellent pastors and teachers. You can find videos on any topic, on any book of the Bible, and by any pastor. You can watch them and use the printable study questions on your own, or you could watch with your spouse or family, or even get a group of friends to watch together and discuss the questions.

You can also just sit down and read the Bible on your own, along with a devotional book or Bible commentary you like. Reading His Words and the accounts of His life is the best way to know Jesus. My mother gave me a simple devotional book called *Time With God: The New Testament for Busy People* twenty-five years ago when I had a two-year-old and a newborn baby.[3] I still read it every day. Now, sitting down with my favorite devotionals and the Bible first thing in the morning with my cup of coffee is my favorite part of the day. God feels like a friend and a Father. When I read His words and write thoughts and prayers in my journal, it feels like I'm having a conversation with Him. I tell Him my problems and concerns, even though He knows them already. It feels like talking to a parent, knowing that He'll be compassionate and understanding, no matter what my concerns are. And what usually happens is that something I read, or something that comes to mind readjusts my thinking completely. It usually comes back to the basics. Just love that person despite the issue, just be thankful instead of complaining, just trust God instead of worrying. Not because we should, but because it's the only way we'll experience peace, contentment, and joy. Reconnecting with God every morning is like charging my phone. And then my day can begin, with a clean slate. I can play to an audience of One.

WHAT I LEARNED

Watch sermons from good pastors. Jamey Dickens's sermon "Three Questions Everyone Has About God" is a great start for anyone who would like to learn more about how to connect with God. Dickens is easy to understand and entertaining. You can find the sermon on North Point's website.[4] You may have a favorite pastor or have heard of pastors who your friends like. You can find any pastor's library of sermons with a quick online search. Andy Stanley, Max Lucado, Jamey Dickens, and Louie Giglio are just a few of my favorites.

Read books written by pastors and teachers. It's helpful to read good authors who can explain how stories from the Bible apply to our lives today. If you haven't read these kinds of books yet, you may want to start with Andy Stanley's books. He is a great communicator and teacher. His sermons and books helped me understand God in a new, better way. He has more than twenty books, and they are easy to read—entertaining too. Author Bob Goff's books are required reading for anyone wanting to learn what it means to be friends with a loving God. His first book is the runaway bestseller *Love Does*.[5] Just read it; you'll thank me later. Everyone who comes to my house gets a copy. You'll love it.

Join a small group at a local church. In most cases you don't have to be a member of the church to join a study or fellowship group. It's more fun to learn alongside others, and it's a great way to meet new friends. Churches' websites will have small-group information available and provide ways for you to reach out and connect.

17

Be Prepared for the Call

Preparing your minds for action, and being sober-minded, set your hope fully on the grace that will be brought to you at the revelation of Jesus Christ.

–1 PETER 1:13 ESV

I'll never forget when Oprah's producer called to ask me to come on their show. Although our publicist Nanette warned me not to ask her about getting on Oprah when we first met, you can't help but hope it will happen. Naturally, we all want some magnificent opportunity to happen immediately to launch our dreams quickly. If a famous celebrity discovered our book and put it on their recommended book list, we'd be set. If a billionaire became enamored with our vision and donated enough money for us to do everything we needed to do, we'd succeed immediately. There are all kinds of scenarios we can imagine that would make our journeys to success easier.

Of course, it would have been wonderful to demonstrate our Coupon Mom system on Oprah's show when we first came out of the gate. But that didn't happen for us. What did happen was that we had eight years of fits and starts, successes and failures, good and bad experiences. We had many media appearances on television news shows. Eight years seemed like forever, but by the time that phone call from Oprah's producer came in, we were ready. We were prepared. Some would say we were lucky.

Do you feel lucky? Or do you feel others are just luckier than you? We see people succeed and wonder why they are doing so well. We might tell ourselves that they just got lucky. Why can't we get a break? Why do we have to work so hard when some have the waters part for them everywhere they go? But if we looked behind their curtain, we might see something different. We might see that they are doing more than just working—they are getting prepared. Do you feel like you're lucky, or do you feel like you keep getting the short end of the stick, despite your hard work?

OPRAH'S OPPORTUNITY

The producer called at 8:30 p.m. on a Wednesday night, October 1, 2008. Looking back on that phone call, it seemed as though the producer was frazzled. She had been in a long meeting with her team. They were trying to plan a special hour-long segment to teach viewers how to handle a financial crisis that threatened the livelihood of millions of Americans—because two days earlier, on September 29, the stock market had crashed. It was the largest single-day drop the stock market had ever had at that time.

Oprah's team scrapped the next week's programming plan and decided to have a special segment on October 8 to teach viewers practical tips for saving money on their household expenses. The team had found a woman in Florida who had helped a local family set up a budget. The Florida mom didn't have a website and she wasn't a professional financial adviser. She was a regular mom, which is what the Oprah team wanted. Fortunately for me, the Florida mom didn't do the grocery coupon thing, and the Oprah team felt that aspect was important. So the producer was searching for someone who could do a dramatically impressive job of saving money at the grocery store. The producer picked up the file our publicist Nanette had provided in case the show ever needed a grocery shopping expert.

Who would call my office line at that late hour on a Wednesday night? Fortunately, I was in my office, so I was there to answer the phone. She told me what they were trying to do and said, "Do you think we can film a shopping trip with you if we come to Atlanta this weekend?" Well, there was only one answer to that question. The TV crew came, we spent the day filming at our local grocery store, and the Oprah team produced an excellent three-minute shopping video. I would go to Chicago the following week to be on the show. They would air the video, then Oprah would ask me a few questions.

It was the luckiest thing that has ever happened to our business.

But here's the thing. The producer didn't call because all the famous celebrities were busy. She didn't call to be nice to me. She called because there was something they needed, and it was something I could provide. If they'd called eight years earlier, doing the shopping trip would have been easy, but our website would never have been able to handle the traffic. A crashed website would have been unprofessional, it would not have met the viewers' needs, and we would have missed the entire opportunity of the "Oprah effect." Fortunately, by October 8, 2008, we had optimized and improved the website to the point where it was bulletproof. It was the perfect combination of opportunity meeting preparation. So yes, we were very lucky.

BE PREPARED FOR OPPORTUNITY

Oprah Winfrey herself has said, "I believe luck is preparation meeting opportunity. If you hadn't been prepared when the opportunity came along, you wouldn't have been lucky."[1]

We don't know what opportunities are around the corner, and when they appear, we may not have time to get ready to handle them. It had taken years of website crashes caused by media coverage for us to know how to make the site bulletproof. Every time you experience a mistake or a bump in the road, you'll become more prepared for the next opportunity. You'll learn and you'll become stronger. Even if it seems like your journey is taking longer than you'd hoped, its timing may be exactly what you need. You're getting stronger, wiser, and more capable. You're getting more prepared for the next opportunity.

When Nanette joined our team, she was very clear in her approach to the media. She simply told them I was the leading expert on saving money on groceries. Well, think about that. Every single household has a person who is their expert on saving money on groceries. Having someone claim to be an expert at such a common practice seems a little brazen. Okay, a lot brazen. But that worked, and she booked many media appearances.

YOU'RE GETTING STRONGER, WISER, AND MORE CAPABLE.

In those short three-to-five-minute interviews, you can only share a few tips. Certainly not everything people need to know, but a few basic tips. And to my surprise, the emails flooded in. Some people did think those tips were helpful. They were new information to them. Not to everyone, but to enough people to make a difference. And that's what we want our new dreams to do—to help enough people to make a difference. When we get positive feedback, we naturally want to continue improving our offering and sharing helpful information with more people. Are you listening to your people? Are you learning from the people you are trying to help?

The key is to become an expert in what you love to do. Don't be intimidated by the word *expert*—you qualify as an expert if you know more than the average person does on your favorite topic. You may have a great deal of knowledge and insight now, but there's always more to learn. By continually learning more in your field, and learning more about what people need, you'll become a sought-after expert and you'll reach far more people. And you'll be getting more prepared for the call.

If you are advising people as an expert in a field, it's important to continue practicing your expertise. That may sound obvious, but sometimes experts get so busy doing interviews, giving talks, writing books, and running the business of being an expert that they may not have time to practice the activity itself. Gardening experts may not have the time to garden, pastors may be too busy pastoring to spend time reading the Bible and praying, professional chefs may not have time to cook meals at home.

When our Coupon Mom website was in its busiest years, I was doing multiple media interviews every day. Our message was that people could cut their grocery bill in half, and they could feed a family of four (or more) a healthy diet for a hundred dollars a week or less. Our family had done that for years, so I knew it was possible. When my husband quit his job to run the household, he took over the meal planning and grocery shopping, if you can believe that.

After a year of his new role, I realized that wasn't right. If I was teaching America how to save money with coupons, it was necessary for *me* to be managing our household with the same hundred-dollar-a-week grocery budget. When I did interviews, the advice would be realistic and practical, based on real obstacles and opportunities I encountered. When an interviewer asked me a question, I could answer with a real savings example I'd used that week for my own family. To stay current, we need to be practicing our own craft as we did before we got so busy being an expert. My learning was continuous, so my advice was authentic and relatable for our audience. It was fun to be able to justify doing my favorite hobby as on-the-job training!

INVESTING FOR FUTURE OPPORTUNITIES

We can spend just an hour per day learning more about our field of interest and become an authority over time, particularly compared to people who know nothing about it. You will be helpful to them by sharing your knowledge via your dream initiative.

What is one hour per day? It's listening to podcasts, watching videos, or reading articles written by other experts in your field. It's reading studies and research papers on your topic. It's talking to real people with experience in your area and talking to the people you are helping. The more you learn, the more confident you'll become as you share your knowledge and others' experience as well. It's your favorite topic, after all, so it's not a chore. It's simply a matter of being intentional. Don't rest on your laurels; continue to get prepared for the call. When it comes, you'll be ready.

It's like our faith journey. It's never finished because it's a relationship with God. If we stay connected with Him as a Father and as a friend, He becomes more real to us. When we spend time reading Scripture, devotionals, and praying every day, we get to know Him better. He already knows us better than anyone else does, and He sees our entire journey at once. He sees who we were, and He sees who we are becoming. Perhaps He uses our journey toward our big dreams to draw us closer to Him. Through the mistakes, the successes, and all the time between them. Could that be how He prepares us? Could that be how He helps us become who He knows us to be?

We are impatient, especially when we want to share something wonderful with the world. We might mean well, we might be working hard, we might have the right motives. So why wouldn't God just snap His fingers and get our big dream off the ground quickly?

Maybe you're frustrated because you've been working a long time and you're almost out of resources. Waiting eight years doesn't work for you. Well, if anyone had told me it would be eight years before the big call came, it would have sounded discouraging too. And if we'd known the Oprah call was coming eventually, we might not have worked as hard at all the other opportunities that came before the call.

> **WE NEED TO KNOW WHY WE'RE WRITING THE STORY IN THE FIRST PLACE.**

That's why it's a good thing we don't have a crystal ball. We don't need to know the end of the story or even the middle of the story. We just need to know why we're writing the story in the first place.

All the opportunities and challenges are important parts of our journey. They get us ready to handle the next call. All our experiences help prepare us for the big thing. It may take ten years, twenty years, or maybe even longer—who knows? But what we can know is that no matter how long it takes, it will have been worth the wait, because during our waiting, we experience our journeys. And it's our journeys that help us become who God wants us to be. Even if our journeys include failures and frustrations, they're part of what strengthens us to respond to that call.

I mentioned that my friend Amanda, who deals with a serious illness, loves God and radiates His love. When we talk about her outlook, she uses the metaphor of getting prepared. She says if she neglects her relationship with God, her supply of love, hope, and joy becomes depleted. When she encounters people who may need some of that, she won't be able to share with them. If she allows herself to become empty, she'll be missing out on the whole reason she believes she is alive. Not just to love others but to share God's love with others. Do you know an Amanda? Are you an Amanda?

Amanda says she focuses on being prepared to share God's love with others, since she never knows who she may encounter. She stays connected to God continually so that His love will naturally flow to any who cross her path. Not because of her efforts, but because God works through her. Because of her serious illness, Amanda expects that she may have limited time here on earth. She says that rather than focusing on that outcome, she decides each day to live intentionally. She views each day as a gift and joyfully anticipates people she may encounter who could be in need of a little love, joy, and hope. She is prepared for today, she is prepared for tomorrow, and she is prepared to meet her Savior. She is prepared for the call. Are we?

WHAT I LEARNED

Start preparing today. Identify how you can become more knowledgeable in your area and craft a plan. Discipline yourself to set aside a certain amount of time every day or week to learn more in your field. Whether it's formal learning or informal conversations with the people you seek to help, you'll become more prepared.

Stay connected to God. Our relationship with God directly impacts our ability to connect with and help others with what we love to do. We never know when we'll have the opportunity to love people the way God wants us to. Being in a relationship with Him is the best preparation we can have.

Don't get discouraged. Every day is another day of training. Your best opportunity may be next week, next year, or ten years from now. The further away it is, the more prepared and successful you'll be when it comes. Don't get discouraged by artificial timelines. When the call comes, it will be the perfect timing.

18

Living with an Attitude of Gratitude

Rejoice always, pray continually, give thanks in all circumstances; for this is God's will for you in Christ Jesus.

—1 THESSALONIANS 5:16-18

nn Voskamp's book *One Thousand Gifts: A Dare to Live Fully Right Where You Are* makes a compelling case for the daily practice of gratitude. Ann is a farmer's wife, a homeschooling mother of six, and a gifted writer. A friend gave me her book when our family was going through a difficult time after our son had an accident. It was heartbreaking to watch him struggle through the pain and loneliness of being stuck in bed for weeks. It's hard enough when we have our own problems, but when we watch people we love go through difficulties we can't fix, it's even harder. Even so, Ann's book opened my eyes to the fact that practicing gratitude every day can change our outlook, bring us peace in the midst of turmoil, and change our lives.

After reading her book, I put her daily gratitude exercise into practice. It really is the best way to experience life—regardless of how difficult our circumstances may be from time to time. It has changed my life, which is why it's worth talking about with you. Perhaps you've already made this discovery, but if not, this may be the best practice you can start. It was for me.

STARTING A GRATITUDE JOURNAL

We've all heard that phrase—*attitude of gratitude*. Maybe that sounds a little Pollyannaish. A little idealistic. We can understand why people talk about gratitude, but they aren't walking through what we're going through. They don't have the difficulties and challenges we have. How in the world are we supposed to have gratitude in the midst of all our problems? It would be better if the problems were solved. Why doesn't God just do that?

Ann's gratitude exercise is simple. She suggests making a list of a thousand things we are thankful for. Hence the title, *One Thousand Gifts*.[1] After reading her book, I got a blank journal and kept it on the nightstand by my bed. Ann carried a small notebook with her throughout the day and noted simple things she noticed and added them to her list. If you want to give this a try, find a simple way to keep track of items to add to your list. It could be a note on your phone where you type or speak onto your list. No matter how we track our gratitude gifts, the key is that it makes us pay attention to the wonderful things we see or experience throughout our days.

Keeping my journal next to my bed works best because it's the last thing I do before going to bed each night. Seeing the journal every night reminds me to record the moments and events of the day that sparked joy, what made me appreciate a friend, who made me feel loved, or moments when I showed someone they were loved. If my journal were on my phone, it would be too easy for it to slip my mind. Doing this daily is the key to establishing a regular routine, so we learn to keep gratitude at the front of our mind. Sitting and remembering the things that happened every night is an uplifting way to end each day. Remembering unexpected conversations or phone calls, pretty sunsets, a big laugh with a friend, or a happy event for one of our children gives me a feeling of gratitude every night.

When we start our journals, Ann recommends writing down every single thing we can think of that we're thankful for. It's easy to get started because we naturally list the big ones. Our families, friends, having food on the table, a roof over our heads, our sweet puppy, our freedom to worship God—the list goes on. For about thirty lines. Then we may get stuck. That's when our daily gratitude items make us see the world differently.

Unlike our routine prayers where we tend to repeat our thanks for these same big items, our gratitude journal gets us to think beyond the big things. We don't need to repeat the big things, since they're already on the list. Each day, we add the smaller things. Knowing that the gratitude journal is waiting at the end of the day makes us more attentive to the smaller things over the course of a day. And when we start paying attention, we realize that they're not small at all. They're what make life interesting.

Looking for our "one thousand gifts" becomes our mission. And when we make that our mission, our outlook changes. Our attitudes change. Our lives change. And hopefully, we'll be helping change the lives of the people in our lives. Hopefully, our gratitude will show up in the love we show for them.

> **OUR GRATITUDE CAN HELP US MOVE ALONG GOD'S JOURNEY MORE EASILY.**

As we proceed on our journey to follow God's path to make a difference in the world, it's easy to get caught up in worrying, striving, or frustration when situations are challenging. When we make gratitude practice a habit, we can catch ourselves before we get derailed by negative thinking. Our gratitude can help us move along God's journey more easily.

INTENTIONAL LIVING

Having a gratitude journal may show you what really matters most to you. Ann Voskamp is a poet, a writer, and a photographer. She is an artist. Her examples of items she'd put on her list included beautiful things she'd seen, such as a scene from nature or even the colors on the soap bubbles in her dishwashing sink. When we pay attention to the world around us, we'll see more reasons to appreciate the beauty that surrounds us, or the people we do life with, or the ideas that matter to us. It's a good way to get to know yourself better, because your list will tell you who you are. It will tell you what your priorities are. When we have a good understanding of our priorities, we can be intentional about spending more of our time on those priorities.

Being more intentional about having gratitude makes us more intentional about living. The people I admire most are very intentional about how they live. That's the key to enjoying life to the fullest. They decide to be grateful. They decide to love God and live in a way that reflects their love for God by loving people. They live each day as if it's their last. They notice what's going on around them rather than rushing through their activities just to get to the next thing. When you talk to them, you feel like you're the only person in the room. They are fully present. The people in their lives feel truly loved. They are filled with gratitude. Is there someone you know who does this well?

Gratitude and intentionality are circular processes. When we start looking for reasons to be thankful and find them, we are really just noticing them. They were always there; we were just rushing by them before. When we start noticing how simple events and interactions brighten our days, we might become more intentional about bringing those moments into others' lives. When we realize how much that unexpected phone call from a friend meant to us, we decide to pick up the phone to make that unexpected call to another person, even if it's a little extra effort. When we realize how much a friendly neighbor's conversation meant when we encountered them on a walk, we stop to talk to more neighbors with genuine interest, even if it takes a little time.

Maybe we'll send thoughtful text messages to more people or be friendlier to strangers we interact with throughout the day. Maybe we'll wake up each morning with anticipation about what unexpected surprises will happen instead of dreading our busy schedules. Maybe we'll wake up each morning being truly thankful that we get another day. After filling more than one gratitude journal by now, I can honestly say that I wake up every day with gratitude. My first thoughts start with being grateful for another day. Throughout the day, it's become a habit to pay attention to see what might happen that could make the gratitude journal that night. It's made me more hopeful, optimistic, and happier. I hope it has made me more loving.

If any of this sounds appealing, give a gratitude journal a try. In just a couple minutes a day of recording happy things in a book, you may experience a change in your overall attitude, happiness, and intentionality in your daily living. I hope so. Try it for thirty days and see if it becomes a habit. What do you have to lose?

Maybe that seems too simple or naive. There are major issues you're dealing with. Keeping a list of happy thoughts isn't going to solve them. That's true. But worrying about the things we can't control won't solve them either. If there was any way to solve them, we would have by now. Worry is what we do when we can't fix things or when we can't control a situation.

One thing I believe: you cannot think two thoughts at once. It's impossible. It's easy for our worrying thoughts to spin around in our minds as we try to come up with ways to solve problems. When we can't solve the problem, worrying is our default. We think there's nothing we can do but worry, but there's still one thing we can do. We may not be able to get rid of those thoughts entirely, but we can try to replace them.

Be intentional with your thoughts. Catch those worrying thoughts and replace them with something at the top of your gratitude list. Stopping to think of something we're thankful for interrupts the worrying thought. When we redirect our thinking to gratitude instead of worry, it's like changing the channel. When we practice this more often, it becomes easier each time. And yes, it does work. It's impossible to worry and be thankful at the same time.

When we're on the gratitude channel, we get one step closer to the peace we so desperately need. We'll most likely go back to the worrying channel, maybe just a few seconds later. And then we try it again. The more we practice this, the better we get at it. The more time we spend on the gratitude channel, the more freedom we have from the worry and anxiety, which never help anyway. The gratitude channel is a much better place to be. Worrying never changes anything, but gratitude can.

Scripture talks about the types of things we can think about to have peace. The list

WORRYING NEVER CHANGES ANYTHING, BUT GRATITUDE CAN.

in Philippians 4:8 includes thinking about whatever is true, noble, right, pure, lovely, admirable, excellent, or praiseworthy. For me it's helpful to come up with specific examples in my life to associate with each adjective, and when a negative or anxious thought is taking up too much real estate in my mind, I visualize one of these words and associated things. Actual examples from my life experience make those words come alive. Everyone's list would be different, but here is mine:

- **Whatever is true:** God's love for us.
- **Whatever is noble:** My brother's integrity in managing our parents' will.
- **Whatever is lovely:** The beauty of nature where we live.
- **Whatever is pure:** Our dog's perpetual happiness whenever he sees any person.
- **Whatever is admirable:** My friend Nanette, who was kind to everyone all the time.
- **Whatever is excellent or praiseworthy:** Rich people who are very generous with their money to help the less fortunate.

What comes to mind when you see these words? Can you think of examples from your life that make these words come alive for you? When I can catch a worrying thought and replace it with the unbelievable reality that this big God loves each of us individually, unconditionally, and nothing will ever change that, that first negative thought gets pushed out of the way. Simply changing the channel to thoughts that bring joy and peace helps us refocus on positive thoughts. We can't complain and be grateful at the same time. So change the channel when you can.

WHAT I LEARNED

Start a gratitude journal. A simple notebook next to your bed will remind you to list all the things you're grateful for each day. You may be surprised at how many there are and how this practice helps you pay more attention to your experiences throughout the day.

Be intentional. Once you notice what surfaces as priorities in your gratitude journal, try to create more of those experiences. Do more of what makes you happy. They may be small things, but it's the small things that add up to a life filled with gratitude.

Change your thought channel. Practice the skill of replacing anxious thoughts with positive thoughts, such as what you are grateful for or what brings you peace. When we get good at this and can do it more often, we'll notice an overall change in our peace and contentment.

19

Unleash the Joy of Giving

God loves a cheerful giver.

—2 CORINTHIANS 9:7

S ince they changed the tax law, donations aren't tax-deductible since we don't itemize," my friend explained. "We can't afford to donate to charity anymore since we can't deduct donations from our taxes." That statement may be logical from a tax standpoint, but no one ever said giving was based in logic.

How much we give away is common discussion, particularly in the faith community. Just this week the topic of money and giving came up in our women's group. It started with the discussion Jesus had with the rich man who asked Jesus how he could have eternal life (Matthew 19:6–30). Jesus told him to sell all that he had and give it to the poor and follow Jesus, and then the man would have treasure in heaven. The man went away sad instead of following Jesus. He was too rich to give it all away. After that conversation,

Jesus turned and explained to His disciples that it is hard for the rich to get into heaven. It would be easier for a camel to get through the eye of a needle than for a rich man to get into heaven.

It's a difficult passage to accept because by the world's standards, we are all very rich. Naturally, we like our comfort and can't imagine giving all our money and possessions away. It would cause us pain and misery, so how could we do that? But maybe that's not exactly what Jesus meant. Perhaps He was trying to tell us that if we could do it, giving generously would actually give us what we needed in our lives. Rather than being a painful sacrifice, it would fill us with joy. And when we experience that joy, we value living out God's love here on this planet more than our comfort and our stuff. It's not about what we have; it's about what matters to us. Where our hearts are, there our treasure is. When we value being generous more than our stuff, we have our treasure in heaven.

The women in our group agreed that giving generously makes sense if we love God, and it's how we show others that God loves them too. That led to the discussion of how much we give. What about tithing? Is giving 10 percent of our income the correct guideline? Is that the rule? And is that percentage based on before-tax or after-tax income? Does this mean that 10 percent of our income needs to go to the

> **IT'S NOT ABOUT WHAT WE HAVE; IT'S ABOUT WHAT MATTERS TO US.**

church and giving to other nonprofits is separate, or does all charitable giving count toward that 10 percent?

LOVING THROUGH GIVING

I wonder what God is thinking when we have these conversations. Fortunately, He's pretty patient with us and probably knows we'll get back on track eventually. We'll remind ourselves it's not about how we give; it's about why we give. It's about our hearts. Are we giving because we love God and want to show love to others? Or are we giving for other reasons that have more to do with how we appear to others or how we measure up to arbitrary standards?

Don't get me wrong; I'm thankful for any giving that people do, regardless of their motivations. Helping the less fortunate for any reason is wonderful. No matter what our motives are, giving helps others, and that's the best part. But if we truly want to love God and love others as Jesus said, we can do a better job loving others by helping them with our giving.

When you are pursuing God's purpose and plan for your life, you may be called to be more generous—with time, money, or both. Responding to God's call to be generous will most likely be the most rewarding part of your journey. Generous and cheerful giving becomes habit-forming in a wonderful way.

I'm all for setting goals for giving. They help us remember to give, and we can build them into our budgets to make sure they happen. But when arbitrary rules or standards make us feel obligated to give, or even resentful of giving, we risk shortchanging ourselves of the joy that God delights in seeing us experience. That joy is what connects our hearts to our giving. That joy reminds us that our true treasure is in heaven. Are you experiencing this joy?

Paul told the Corinthians that our giving causes others to give thanks to God (2 Corinthians 9:11). Think about that. When we give generously to someone in need, they may have been praying desperately for a solution to their problem or crisis. When our unexpected gift eases their pain, when it solves their problem, they can't help but be thankful to God. And in that experience, their faith in God increases. They are reminded that this big God of the universe didn't forget about them. They feel loved by God, and generosity is the tool God used to remind them of His love. We get to do that. How can we not be filled with joy when we understand our role in that transaction? How can our hearts not be changed?

When our hearts are changed, we look at the world differently. Instead of feeling obligated to give, we can ask God to show us where and when to give. When we start paying attention to opportunities to respond to where God needs us to give, we are in a position to receive the gifts God wants us to find. It's surprising how clearly opportunities present themselves when we view being able to help others as a gift God gives us. And when we know our giving is an answer to God's prayer for someone, when we know He is prompting us to help in a situation, our joy grows exponentially when we respond to that call. It's actually addictive. Once we've experienced being included in God's transaction, we can't help but watch and wait for the next one. Can you think of a time you knew you were part of God's answer to someone else's prayer for help?

In God's economy, the size of our gifts isn't what matters the most, it's our hearts that matter. We can love others generously with small gifts as well as large gifts. We can give generously with our time and talents as well as with our money. Everyone, regardless of financial constraints, can be a part of this great big, wonderful plan of God's. To give so others will give thanks to God. Don't feel like you must sit on the sidelines if you aren't a millionaire. You have all kinds of gifts that can help. Sharing them will fill you with joy. What gifts can you share?

> **YOU HAVE ALL KINDS OF GIFTS THAT CAN HELP.**

GIVING OUT OF GUILT?

In the story of Jesus and the rich young man, the rich man walked away sad after he heard Jesus' answer. We can imagine that he even felt guilty about not being able to let go of his wealth. Why did God give us so much when we see so many others in the world and even in our communities suffering from poverty? Why wouldn't we feel guilty?

Sarah Young addresses this in her devotional book *Jesus Calling*, writing about her imagined perspective of how Jesus would speak to us on this topic: "Sometimes My children hesitate to receive My good gifts with open hands. Feelings of false guilt creep in, telling them they don't deserve to be so richly blessed. This is nonsense-thinking because no one deserves anything from Me. My kingdom is not about earning and deserving; it's about believing and receiving."[1]

Years ago, a friend shared the phrase *blessed to be a blessing* with me. She explained that God blesses us with all that we have, and then we have the option to bless others with what He has given us. In that process, we experience joy. We experience fulfillment because we know we're doing God's work here on earth. We are His arms and legs. We're sharing His love with our generosity because God was generous with us. When we give, we will be blessed. We'll be blessed with joy and fulfillment. We'll be blessed to be a blessing.

Some of my friends believe when we give to others, God will bless us with more. If we give money, He will give us more money. This is when we get tripped up. When we start thinking that we earn and deserve what we have, or when we think we should give money so we can get more money, we start spinning in circles. We get confused when we expect our giving will lead to God giving us more money. Scripture says He will bless us when we give, and He does. He blesses us with wonderful gifts like joy, fulfillment, contentment, peace, and love. We can't put a price on the value of those blessings. He already blessed us with money; that's why we can give. He gives us the gift of being able to experience giving.

When we think of giving as a privilege God gives us, it changes our perspective. There are many ways God could answer someone's prayer for help, including giving them what they need through another means. Instead, He chose us to be the one included in their story. He chose us to experience that joy. He's giving us the lead part in His story, and all we have to do is accept it. No tryouts required.

GUIDELINES FOR GIVING

So how do we give? What does it mean to watch for God's opportunities to give? In our group's discussion about how to measure giving, we only talked in terms of giving to tax-deductible places of worship or nonprofit organizations. Perhaps the most important change I've experienced in giving has been my perspective on this. Yes, giving to nonprofit organizations doing great work is important. When a group of dedicated people are working effectively to help others, we're thankful they give us an easy way to help simply by supporting them. We don't have to start our own organizations but can encourage them and help grow their efforts with our financial support. They make it easy for us.

But if we limit our giving based on tax-deductibility, we may miss out on being a part of God's answer to someone's prayer. Giving directly to a person in need is not tax-deductible, but it can be life-changing. Not just for them, but for us. When you feel God's nudge to help an individual, don't let the tax-deductibility issue be a showstopper. That's not a dead end; that's just math.

Here's the math. Let's suppose your top tax rate is 35 percent when you combine federal and state rates. That means if you itemize your taxes and donate one hundred dollars to a charity, you'll get thirty-five dollars off your taxes, so your

WE MAY MISS OUT ON BEING A PART OF GOD'S ANSWER TO SOMEONE'S PRAYER.

actual cost will be sixty-five dollars. Some people think when a donation is tax-deductible, it doesn't cost them anything. Some people think that if a donation isn't tax-deductible, they can't afford it.

Even if you don't itemize your taxes because the standard exemption—which has risen for many filers in recent years—makes more sense for you, the reality is that if you can afford to give a charity one hundred dollars when you could deduct donations, then you can afford to give sixty-five dollars to charity without being able to deduct it from taxes. The final net cost of each gift would be sixty-five dollars. That's enough math for now because you get my point. If our concern is not being able to afford a gift, we can simply adjust the final number if we need to. My guess is once we experience the joy of changing an individual's situation, we won't be doing the math at all. The personal connection we experience in giving will become far more important than the math.

Years ago, our children's school bus driver had a financial crisis, and a few of us heard that her electricity had been turned off. Miss Sharon was adored by all the children and parents because she was loving and kind to each child. She had been the neighborhood bus driver for years. It was heartbreaking to hear that she was suffering. I was the community service person on the PTA, so I asked the principal for permission to send out a flyer to families requesting support for her—anonymously, of course. The flyer simply said that we wanted to raise money for a school staff member who was experiencing a financial challenge.

The initial response to the flyer's request was minimal. Some people sent in small contributions, which was nice. Then somehow, word got out that the anonymous staff member was actually our beloved Miss Sharon. Once that anonymous person had a face and a name, many parents' hearts broke. Just as with statistics, when our giving becomes personal, all bets are off. The money flooded in. Neighbors with children who had graduated from Miss Sharon's bus route years earlier called, asking how they could help.

We ended up giving Miss Sharon thousands of dollars, clothing, groceries, gas cards, Christmas gifts for her family, and more. Most important, we showed Miss Sharon how dearly loved she was. In all likelihood, we helped answer her prayers to God, which was His idea all along. No one got a tax deduction—no one even asked. When our hearts get involved, math goes out the window. Exactly where it belongs. We ended up forming a Sharon Cares team and provided ongoing support for her in many ways. And we were filled with joy.

What if we didn't do any math at all? What if we didn't set a limit on our giving with a percentage? What if we didn't make tax-deductibility a requirement? What if we just paid attention to however God nudged us to help? Our family doesn't have a percentage goal for giving. We did in the past, and we found that when we hit that number, we stopped giving. We stopped paying attention. It felt like an insurance deductible. We file taxes and include the tax-deductible contributions, of course. I am a Coupon Mom, after all. But we don't add that up until tax time. We can't tell you how much we've given or what our percentage is until then, because we don't want to miss God's next opportunity. If we missed it, I believe God would answer that person's prayer with someone else. He can answer anyone's prayer however He wants to. But if He picks me, I don't want to miss the joy of being in His story.

WHAT I LEARNED

Set up intentional giving. If you know the organizations or place of worship you'd like to support, make giving automatic by setting it up in your bank account. At a minimum you'll be sure the charities you care about get your support.

Pray for God to show you where to give. When we watch and wait for opportunities to help and give, it's surprising how clearly they appear. Maybe those are God's nudges, or maybe they are a result of our increased awareness. Take advantage of those opportunities and see what happens.

Know your math. When we give from the heart, we're less concerned about rules. But it does make sense to keep track of charitable contributions since you can take them as deductions on your tax return if you qualify. You'll be stretching the power of your dollars to help others. Consult with your tax adviser on whether you can deduct charitable contributions in accordance with your tax situation.

Conclusion

IMAGINE TOGETHER

Most of us are dreamers.

Some of us will decide to take steps to achieve our dreams. Others will not. If you feel a nudge to look for your dream, or to start taking steps toward a dream you have had for a long time, I hope you follow it. Begin to notice your own story and ask God to help you discover the beautiful one He has in mind for you, one that is ideally suited for your life situation. You may not know exactly what it is right now, and that is okay. Just look for that first small step and go from there. You don't need permission from anyone else, and you don't need a consensus. You can just start.

It can be lonely to be a dreamer, particularly in the first few steps. More than twenty years ago, when I started taking the first steps toward my dream, I noticed an ad on the lid of my yogurt cup about an essay contest for people who were starting charitable endeavors. The prize was $2,000, and the essay requirement was five hundred words. Your favorite charity would receive $1,000, and you could use $1,000 to fund your own charitable endeavor. At four dollars a word if you were the winner, that contest sounded like a pretty good deal to me.

To my surprise, I won. I used the prize money to buy a computer and chose North Fulton Community Charities to receive $1,000, since they had shown me so much support and encouragement. As excited as I was about the money, the validation of my idea was even more meaningful. The small grant was a giant boost to my confidence and helped spur my idea along.

Today my dream is to help provide this kind of encouragement to dreamers, because I know how powerful it is to have complete strangers believe in your idea. I hope your family and friends are cheering you on. But when someone you don't even know believes in your vision enough to send you a check, it's amazing. Because I know the power of financial support, 100 percent of my proceeds from this book will be given as small grants to dreamers through our Imagine More program.

As you begin your journey toward God's plan for your dream, consider joining our Imagine More community to support you. I hope Imagine More will become a community of friends who are following God together. We can provide grants to dreamers, learn useful skills from subject experts, communicate with one another, and celebrate each other's progress toward our dreams. There are so many possibilities for what Imagine More could become with all of you involved, and I look forward to watching it unfold. Simply go to www.stephanienelson.com/imaginemore and sign up to apply for our grants, ask questions, share stories, and more. One thing I know for certain—whatever happens together will be immeasurably more than we can imagine right now, because "God can do immeasurably more than we ask or imagine" (Ephesians 3:20).

Let's imagine more.

Acknowledgments

Thank you to God for continuing to surprise me with unexpected adventures. I'm still learning that God's never done with us, and if we pay attention, we will see His new and exciting paths to follow. The process of writing and publishing this book has been a true delight, because I've met so many wonderful people who have become friends. I've learned valuable lessons from all of them. You know who you are—thank you so much. I'd like to mention a few.

Thank you to author Bob Goff. Reading your books shifted my life perspective, and when I went to your writer's workshop in 2021, I was just hoping to meet you. Your encouragement, coaching, and inspiration gave me a new purpose and an exciting new adventure. Most importantly, you have shown me what it looks like to really love people well. To love like Jesus. I am so grateful for you.

Thank you to Mark Gottlieb. You saw what I didn't see. Thank you for taking the bold and brave step of representing my book and for getting it to Thomas Nelson Books. I will always be grateful to you for this.

Thank you to the team at Thomas Nelson Books. I have

never worked with a nicer group of people who live their faith in their daily jobs. Jenny Baumgartner—you are an angel. I don't think it's a coincidence that my book landed on your desk. I am so thankful for you and your faith in the project from the very beginning. Janet Talbert, I appreciated your sweet affirmation and encouragement throughout the whole project. Thank you to the entire Nelson team who made this happen: Andrew Stoddard, Claire Drake, Sarah Van Cleve, Lisa Beech, Natalie Nyquist, and everyone involved on this project.

Thank you to all my friends and family who read chapters and gave feedback early in the process. I'm thankful to the many new friends I met at The Oaks workshops for their encouragement. Thank you to Jamie Chavez for her expertise and affirmation. And to the guests who have come on my *Pivotal People* podcast—they've taught me so much and inspired me to become more like each of them. I appreciate the countless people who came alongside me during the Coupon Mom journey—many of their stories are in the pages of this book.

And finally, thank you to my husband, Dave. After thirty-two years, you are still the best deal I've ever found.

Notes

Chapter 1: The Coupon Mom Story

1. *Good Morning America*, "Easy Coupon Clipping Plan Can Save You Big," featuring Stephanie Nelson, aired on April 29, 2004, on ABC News, https://abcnews.go.com/GMA /AmericanFamily/story?id=127692&page=1.

2. Joseph, "The Extraordinary CMS: WordPress History, Facts, and Stats," FastComet, May 15, 2022, fastcomet.com/blog /wordpress-history-and-statistics.

Chapter 2: Find Your Bold Vision

1. *Your Move with Andy Stanley*, "Re:Solution: Part 1, The Better Question," featuring Andy Stanley, aired on January 24, 2018, on NBC and CBS, 28:25, https://yourmove.is/videos /the-better-question-part-1/.

2. Blake Mycoskie, *Start Something That Matters* (New York: Spiegel & Grau, 2011), 32–33.

3. Damli Mirembe, "Ep. 13: Damali Mirembe: Saving Orphans in Uganda," April 26, 2022, in *Pivotal People*, produced by Stephanie Nelson, podcast, streaming MP3, 26:09, https:// pivotalpeople.buzzsprout.com/1909281/10464612-ep-13 -damali-mirembe-saving-orphans-in-uganda.

Chapter 4: Finding Your Big Idea

1. Reid Hoffman, *Masters of Scale: Surprising Truths from the World's Most Successful Entrepreneurs* (New York: Currency, 2021), 54.
2. David A. Shaywitz, "'Masters of Scale' Review: Make It and 'Blitz' It," *Wall Street Journal*, September 15, 2021, https://www.wsj.com/articles/masters-of-scale-review-make-it-and-blitz-it-11631746266.
3. "Find the Big Idea (Spanx's Sarah Blakely)," day two of a ten-day course, Masters of Scale (app), streaming MP3, 9:59, https://app.mastersofscale.com/content-item/SflifTJW db2nvpdrhfap.
4. Sara Blakely, "How I Built It: Spanx," *Wall Street Journal*, September 16, 2010, https://www.wsj.com/video/how-i-built-it -spanx/D1B6CA1F-819E-4FFB-BCE1-7E437BBB951E.html.

Chapter 5: Rejection: Recalculating Your Route

1. Diane Negra and Su Holmes, eds., *In the Limelight and Under the Microscope: Forms and Functions of Female Celebrity* (New York: Bloomsbury Publishing, 2011), 120, https://www.google.com/books/edition/In_the_Limelight _and_Under_the_Microscop/qzOXAwAAQBAJ.
2. "Meryl Streep 'Not Pretty Enough' to Be in King Kong," *The Graham Norton Show*, January 9, 2015, YouTube video, 2:07, https://www.youtube.com/watch?v=GW0PMN6VAlg.
3. "Meryl Streep—Awards," IMDb, accessed March 28, 2023, https://www.imdb.com/name/nm0000658/awards.

Chapter 6: The Power of Encouragement: My Do-Over

1. J. T. Harding, *Party Like a Rockstar* (New York: Twelve, 2022), quoted in Brian McCollum, "J. T. Harding Tells the Story Behind a Massive Michigan-Made Hit: Uncle Kracker's 'Smile,'" *Detroit Free Press*, February 20, 2022, https://www.freep.com/story/entertainment/music/brian

-mccollum/2022/02/20/j-t-harding-reveals-songwriting-story
-behind-uncle-krackers-smile/6844497001/.
2. Matt Kempner, "Coupon Mom Feeds the Hungry and
Makes Money," *Atlanta Journal–Constitution*, August 25,
2014, https://www.ajc.com/business/coupon-mom-feeds-the
-hungry-and-makes-money/OqQVTR0VlwBwlCQ8H4aO4K/.

Chapter 9: Unsung Heroes: The Coupon Mom Team
1. Tim Schurrer, *The Secret Society of Success: Stop Chasing
the Spotlight and Learn to Enjoy Your Work (and Life)
Again* (Nashville: Nelson Books, 2022), 65–66.

Chapter 10: Fear: If You Don't Feel Capable, Join the Club
1. Deuteronomy 31:6; Joshua 1:9; Psalm 23:4; 27:1; 118:6;
Isaiah 41:10, 13; Philippians 4:6–7.

Chapter 11: Ask for Help and Share the Success
1. Jade Scipioni, "IT Cosmetics Jamie Kern Lima: 'I Lived
Completely Burnt Out for Almost a Decade,'" CNBC,
updated March 20, 2021, https://www.cnbc.com/2021/03/09
/it-cosmetics-jamie-kern-lima-on-building-a-billion-dollar
-company.html.

Chapter 12: Two Words: Kindness Matters
1. Louie Giglio, "The Book of Colossians: Session One—
Colossians 1:1–14," RightNow Media, 2018, streaming
video, 13:00, https://app.rightnowmedia.org/en/content
/details/287526?session=287527.
2. Margaret Renkl, "Ann Patchett Is on Another Roll,"
Chapter 16, April 19, 2012, https://chapter16.org/ann
-patchett-is-on-another-roll/.

Chapter 13: Use God's Yardstick to Measure Success
1. Tim Schurrer, *The Secret Society of Success: Stop Chasing
the Spotlight and Learn to Enjoy Your Work (and Life)
Again* (Nashville: Nelson Books, 2022), 55–58.

2. Sandra Stanley, *Comparison Trap: A 28-Day Devotional for Women, Choosing Contentment in an Age of Awareness* (Atlanta: North Point Resources, 2015).

Chapter 14: You Can't Take the Elevator to Success; You Have to Take the Stairs

1. "History of Rally Foundation," Rally Foundation for Childhood Cancer Research, accessed March 30, 2023, https://rallyfoundation.org/history/.
2. Jack Canfield, "Free Web Event with Jack Canfield," webinar, streamed in August 2021, http://jackcanfieldwebevent.com/.
3. Canfield, webinar.

Chapter 15: Just One Person

1. *Unstuck*, "Session 4: Unstuck," featuring Mark Batterson, hosted by Francis Chan, aired 2013, on RightNow Media, streaming MP3, 31:00, https://app.rightnowmedia.org/es /content/details/476?session=3758.
2. Mercy House Global, accessed April 5, 2023, https://mercy houseglobal.org/#.
3. *Unstuck*, "Session 4: Unstuck."
4. Kristen Welch, "Ep. 18: Kristen Welch—Author and Founder of Mercy House Global," June 7, 2022, in *Pivotal People*, produced by Stephanie Nelson, podcast, streaming MP3, 34:38, https://pivotalpeople.buzzsprout.com/1909281/10748768-ep -18-kristen-welch-author-founder-of-mercy-house-global.

Chapter 16: Playing to an Audience of One: Know Your Audience

1. Amanda Ferrin, "Ep. 3: Amanda Ferrin: Living with Genuine Hope & Joy," January 13, 2022, in *Pivotal People*, produced by Stephanie Nelson, podcast, streaming MP3, 36:48, https:// pivotalpeople.buzzsprout.com/1909281/9884104-ep-3 -amanda-ferrin-living-with-genuine-hope-joy.

2. Jamey Dickens, "3 Questions Everyone Has About God: Part 1, Question One: Who Is He?," September 22, 2019, in *North Point Community Church*, produced by North Point Community Church, podcast, streaming MP3, 36:22, https://omny.fm/shows/north-point-community-church /3-questions-everyone-has-about-god-part-1-jamey-di?in _playlist=podcast.

3. *Time With God: The New Testament for Busy People* (Dallas: Word Bibles, 1992).

4. Dickens, "3 Questions."

5. Bob Goff, *Love Does: Discover a Secretly Incredible Life in an Ordinary World* (Nashville: Thomas Nelson, 2014).

Chapter 17: Be Prepared for the Call

1. Oprah, "Thought for Today—Luck," OWN, March 19, 2010, https://www.oprah.com/spirit/thought-for-today-luck.

Chapter 18: Living with an Attitude of Gratitude

1. Ann Voskamp, *One Thousand Gifts: A Dare to Live Fully Right Where You Are* (Grand Rapids, MI: Zondervan, 2011).

Chapter 19: Unleash the Joy of Giving

1. Sarah Young, *Jesus Calling: Enjoying Peace in His Presence* (Nashville: Thomas Nelson, 2004), s.v. "November 12."

About the Author

S tephanie Nelson is the founder of the Coupon Mom website, which launched the coupon movement that took America by storm in 2008. As a savings expert, Stephanie has appeared on many national and local television news shows, including *Good Morning America*, the *Today* show, and *The Oprah Winfrey Show*. Her entrepreneurial Coupon Mom concept started a national cottage industry of other "coupon moms," as she inspired women to start profitable websites in their communities. Her book *The Coupon Mom's Guide to Cutting Your Grocery Bills in Half* was a *New York Times* bestseller. Stephanie currently hosts her podcast, *Pivotal People*.

To download the bonus resource PDF, *Imagine More Savings: Digital Hacks*, please scan the below QR code with your phone's camera.